The Choices of Criticism

The Choices of Criticism

William Chace Greene

The M.I.T. Press
The Massachusetts Institute of Technology
Cambridge, Massachusetts, and London, England

Library of Congress Catalog Card Number 65–26664
Printed in the United States of America

Preface

This small book began as a series of informal essays trying to express the conclusions of a good many years of talking about criticism. My next-door colleague, Roy Lamson, suggested they were more like lectures than like essays, and through his suggestion and the kindness of John Burchard and Howard Bartlett they were given in the fall of 1962 as five lectures under the sponsorship of the Department of Humanities at the Massachusetts Institute of Technology. Since that time they have been redone, and the "you" of the lecture has become the "he" and the "one" of the essay, whether with any real gain I am not sure.

It will come clear, I fancy, to those who read these chapters that I have some sort of critical position. I have, however, tried to keep it suppressed in the spirit of Rudyard Kipling's relativistic adage: "There are nine and forty ways of writing tribal lays and every single one of them is right." I found in trying to reduce all that I wanted to say to what I could speak out in five fifty-minute lectures that the simplicity and conciseness I had to practice seemed good to me. I have added, perhaps padded, since, but though I cannot boast of many "telling phrases," I can hope I have avoided too much reiteration of idea and elaboration of language.

Various people have given help and some have given criticism. I suppose my major debt, however, lies to those ladies who typed and retyped and often corrected my negligences: Mrs. Bettie Currier, Mrs. Marilyn Silva, and Mrs. Helen Maciel. And, of course, a teacher always owes a debt he cannot measure to the skepticism and insight of the students who try to understand how he would like them to feel and think and speak and write. More formal and impersonal debts are expressed under the figures and in the notes.

William Chace Greene

Cambridge, Massachusetts
August, 1965

Contents

CHAPTER 1

Introduction

WHEREVER we dig up the human past, wherever we run on men today, we find things men have made more fancy than use demands: tools, weapons, pots, clothes, jewelry, hairdos, skin decoration, mats, houses, furniture, dance masks, amulets, gravestones, effigies of totems and ancestors and deities. The range of decorated things is enormous, and few groups of men past and present do not show samples of a great part of it. I remember seeing an anthropologist's film of Australian primitives, a nomadic people who traveled in small family groups, their whole possessions a few carved pots, a few spears, and no clothes at all. At a season of the year the families gathered in some low mountains; the older men circled about the head man, perhaps the oldest, and from a hiding place among the rocks he took a piece of stone on which were carved two spirals. According to the anthropologist's explanatory voice, the old man told a long story of tribal history, using the spirals as tracks of tribal journey, pointing "here this happened, here our hero grandfather did this." Perhaps we can assume, then, that spoken stories are as basic as formed artifacts. And since all people make organized noises of some kind, we can assume music likewise original.

Our own lives pass among made things. What we make we try to make pleasant, good, fine, "nice": our experiences differ, our ideas of the good differ, but the urge toward something more than use requires seems fundamental. We shall have, then, to define art first as the unnecessary addition of attractiveness.

Let us take here a bowl (Figure 1). It is an old bowl made toward 1500 A.D. in Arizona. It was made, we can assume, by a Pueblo Indian woman, for women were the pot-makers of Pueblo tribes. It was made to hold meal or grain. It was decorated. Why? Perhaps in this particular case because a decorated bowl could be traded for more

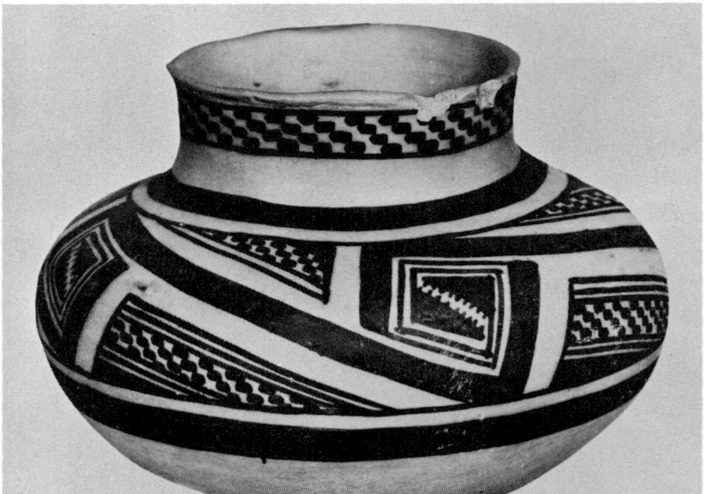

FIGURE 1. Jar from Homolovi, Arizona. Courtesy of the Chicago Natural History Museum. (Illustrated in Martin and Willis, *Anasazi Painted Pottery,* Field Museum of Natural History, Chicago, 1940)

meat or grain or wool than an undecorated one, an economic reason, but this only throws the artistic reason onto the feeling of the "buyer" who was willing—why?—to give more for a decorated pot than an undecorated one. Perhaps, contrariwise, it was decorated only because the pot-maker wanted to decorate it: she was an "artist" for her own satisfaction: she was her own audience.

In the situation of this bowl, then, there are two primary factors, the bowl-maker and the bowl, and a third, not inescapable but at last the most important, those who looked at the bowl in the past and those who look now: artist, art, audience. The bowl came by the mind and hand of the Indian woman; it came, we shall say, out of her experience. What the artist does with the material of art is to give it shape. Shape is both for use—here to hold something and to stand on its bottom and to allow one to lift it—and for some satisfaction of eye and feeling. The bowl is given shape, and so the bowl is given decoration, not haphazard but organized and internally related. No piece of art, you will find, lacks organization of some sort and of some degree. However accidental some painters have tried to make their splashes and their lines, art is not accidental like "life." The mark of a piece of art seems to me to be its unnatural order.

Experience and order come to be two basic words for art. But an area cannot be defined by two lines, and the area of art needs a third word. This one can only come out of the way art is looked at. The bowl can be looked at as an article useful to hold things. It can also be looked at, by the same person and in the next second, as an article nice to look at. Here it has no use beyond its attraction. It is not a thing for something else but a thing for itself, in itself. It is, so seen—and this, it seems to me, is the artistic way to see it—self-sufficient. It needs no other purpose than to be—and to be seen.

If the three words are put together, they make a definition: "art is the self-sufficient ordering of experience." The connotations of the definition will not be immediately plain, perhaps; there is more to say and some insecurity of argument in defense of these characteristics, for few definitions turn out to be absolute, not even in science. Let us, however, rest for the moment here with these three words.

Other men than the maker look at the bowl and say things about it. We can guess at a caveman saying, "I like that bison he painted." And we can then guess at a companion's query in any tone of voice you wish to give it, "You do? Why?" The first man expressed a taste; the second demanded defense of that taste. When the first man went on to say, "Because—" he had taken up criticism, a habit as old as art. And criticism is the subject of this book.

Criticism may seem subjective and niggling and parasitic, and perhaps we should give more honor to the artist than to the critic, for the art is what we enjoy at last. Yet the critic is necessary to the artist. It is out of criticism that the artist grows; it is out of criticism that the public who are not artists form taste, opinion, feelings not only about art but about their lives and attitudes toward action. The early and primitive critic was showing the artist how to be better at his trade; the late critic is creating—for himself, for those who listen to him, and even, indirectly, for those who do not listen to him—a philosophy of human existence. And we are all critics. The crowds pouring from the theaters, the new greater crowds at last turning off their television sets, all comment good or no good, like or not like. No matter how insecure their judgments, they are acting as critics, as they do when they buy lamps or rugs or neckties or flowers for the garden.

The reason for discussing the nature and methods of criticism is in part the improvement of criticism and the improvement of art. "Improvement," I suspect, can only mean greater consistency, logic, being all of a piece. Criticism, however, does more than improve art, for one of the characteristics of the criticism we are inclined to call good is that it implies a thorough view of life as well as a peculiar sensitiveness to art. More thoughtful criticism will, we think, lead to more thoughtful views of action and more justified feelings about men, for what the critic is at bottom always discussing is the viability of art, what feelings it sanctions, what logic it shows, what relation these have to life at large. Many of us—from reading, from picture-gazing, from moviegoing, from staring at our houses and our furniture—test against our opinions the proposals of artists, what they present as good or bad or likely or unlikely. Our acceptances and rejections herein shape us quite as much as our physical, "actual," experiences in life. What we "like" is an expression of us, and by liking we alter or confirm what we were. Criticism, then, which puts thought upon taste, can hardly help enlarging our opinions and our attitudes and our feelings. It has taken me a great number of years to come to the expression of this faith in criticism, but now it seems to me just to phrase that faith, and this discussion will serve in part to show the reasons for it.

Men seem, then, to need art, however some of them scorn it, and they insist on talking about it. The different arts may not seem much alike, for nonverbal music is a long way from verbal story and the dance from the flower garden, yet in a very general way what they each evoke may bear some sort of likeness. And before we can take up the discussion of criticism we must try to find what very general likenesses these are.

Criticism becomes, then, first of all the analysis of a piece of art to uncover its kind of experience and order and self-sufficiency, but it becomes after that some evaluation of these factors, how much, how satisfactory, how good. Underlying these judgments must be a series of criteria of what makes the good in art, and underlying these criteria will lie the philosophic criteria of what makes the good in life.

Such are the materials of this discussion, though it will take some time to get to the end of them. I propose, I think, no ultimate and absolute system, for various men have various views of the good and the proper and the effective and of the purposes of human life, and, as I shall attempt to show, criteria for art depend upon views of these purposes. There can be many sorts of critic; in the old phrase of the marketplace of ideas each one of us may listen, estimate, and come to his own conclusions. The kinds of ideas that must be examined, the necessity of looking at what logically follows what, the range of possible thoughts, so far as I can myself see that range—to look at these is the only proposal I should make. Hence the title of this discussion is "The Choices of Criticism."

CHAPTER 2

The Experience of the Artist

WHAT an artist begins with is a subject, a particular thing he writes about, makes, pictures, or ramifies into a composition. He may come on his subject fresh: while reading a myth he may exclaim, "There's a story I could make out of that!" Or he may work with a long-known subject, like the Buddha Maitreya or the fishing wharf known as "Motif No. 1" at Rockport or an old man who gives his property away to his ungrateful daughters. The subject will define the piece of art, of course, and will limit the experience the artist uses and the audience ultimately enjoys. By the time the work is begun, however, the very subject matter will be part of the artist's experience; and since there are good pictures of "Motif No. 1" and bad ones, the subject matter will not be so much what the art is as the way it is handled, the experience of the artist that has been called on to make the art. Much the same may be said of the materials the artist uses: words, colors, shapes, sounds; they limit what the artist can do—only a limited kind of music is possible with words—but they are at best less important than what has been made by them.

It is true that we often go through a picture to the scene it pictures; we go through the picture of the Holy Family to the Holy Family itself. Yet, even so, it is what the artist has done with his subject that we find *as* the Holy Family —unless we daydream beyond the picture. Thus, I think it possible still to say that art begins from the artist's experience and that this is what he works with.

The lives of artists do not suggest that they need pass through the objective experiences they picture. A great part of the art made during the history of mankind has been religious art: songs, dances, hymns, regalia, vessels, wands, statues, amulets, myths and the ceremonies they explain, and so on. The sentiments from which these derived were genuine sentiments, and many heroes of myth perhaps at one time existed, as saints no doubt existed, as Buddha and Jesus did. Yet no one, I think, would wish to maintain of such a statue of Buddha as this that it wholly or in any great part represented objective experience that the artist had undergone (Figure 2). The artist carved, not even what he thought Buddha might have looked like, but what he thought Buddha ought to have looked like, what he thought Buddha ought to represent in character. Much of lay art has as little foundation in the artist's life: all of Shakespeare's plays, for instance, most of Renaissance painting, most of Greek sculpture and some of Greek vase painting, and in our time many stories, plays, pictures. Music, though its effect has more likeness to life than we may at first think, is unable to imitate action very closely and can only symbolize it. True, the "Pilgrims' Chorus" in *Tannhäuser* gives the effect of a singing group of men approaching, passing, and going on, but I doubt that one would insist Wagner must have had the experience of such a procession. Honegger's *Pacific 231* could hardly be anything but a railroad locomo-

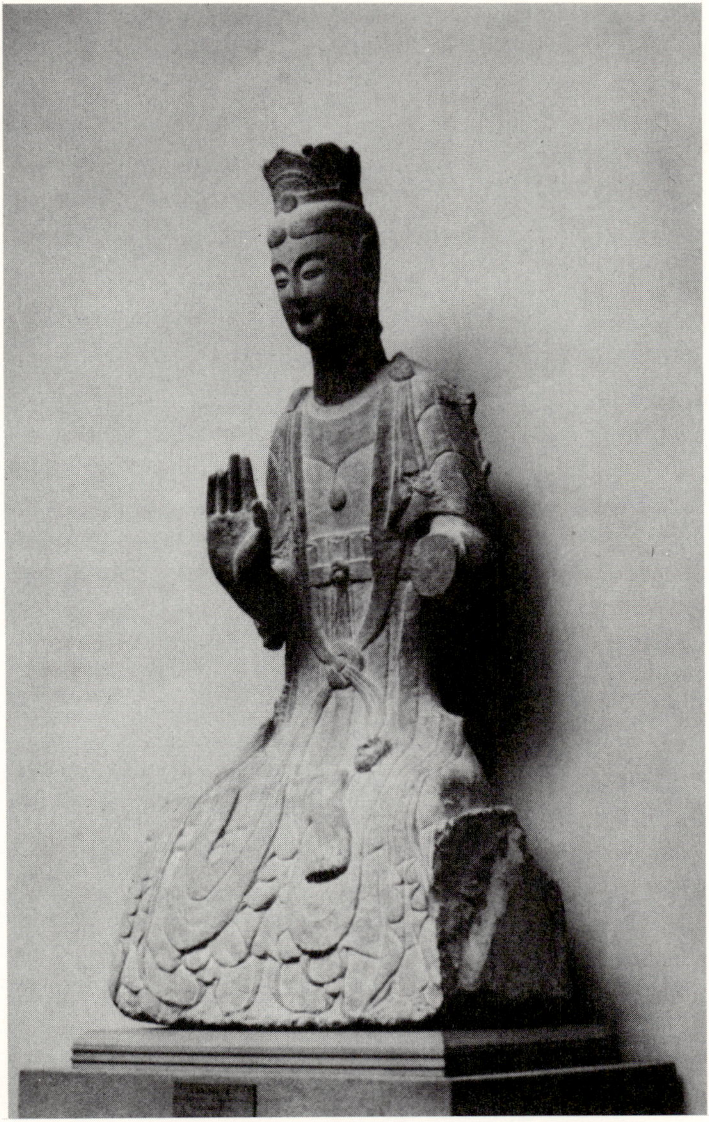

FIGURE 2. The Buddha "Maitreya," Chinese, sixth or seventh century. Courtesy of the Museum of Fine Arts, Boston

tive—unless a hippopotamus getting up in the morning—and we would think it unlikely that anyone who had not heard a locomotive could have composed it, but it is no extraordinary experience, and it is a stunt piece of music at best.

Yet the artist must have experience. If we return to the Indian woman pot-maker, we can imagine some of what she must have had. There had been before her other pot-makers, many other pots, and pots of this shape. Thus, much of the pot-maker's experience was her tribe's past experience: general pot shape, even the habit of painted designs and the particular kind of designs, derived not from "nature" but from the straight line and the triangle. The tribal tradition, of course, put confines around what she could think of doing; she had never seen a Chinese vase and could not imagine it. Yet she saw around her what bowls were, and she had, by the time she started this one, herself made bowls before. All this past was her experience, and most of it craft experience. In a sense, then, the pot is a tribal pot, a community's pot; and indeed most pieces of art, from Madonnas to Argyle socks, are the products of a community's past decision.

She was an individual artist, however, and as she began this bowl, she may have thought of a better bowl, so that in her experience was already an idea. As she molded the coils of clay and smoothed them, she may have felt the value of a slight straightening of the outward curve of her bowl. She may have felt the relation of the neck to the bowl in a new way. Her hands moved, pushed, shaped, tried, rejected, tried, accepted. She was not a machine which duplicates but an inventor who made no two bowls alike, who experimented, who thought out ahead and during, who tried for some perfection, who made choices. And as with shape, so with decoration.

Her experience, then, was of pots, her past, her idea ahead, the working out during the actual fabrication. Her experience was not something else than pots, not experience imitated in this pot—except, of course, her whole feeling, her taste, is somehow here expressed. And at this point, when we ask why she rejected some slight shifts of shape and accepted others, why she put her design on the pot as she did, we have to use another vague and general word, "character." Her experience somehow organized itself into an individual person, and what she made will show that character.

She, of course, was only a maker of pots, demanding very little variety of knowledge. Suppose we try to invent the mind of Shakespeare. Many people have been unable to reconcile what we know of Shakespeare's life with the depth and diversity of his knowledge of men. There are no records of "dramatic" events in his life: he was acquainted with other playwrights and with other stage folk; we guess from his plays that he had acquaintance with country folk and with city tavern dwellers; arrested for poaching by his next-door neighbor, Sir Thomas Lucy, he knew the kind of local knight who became Justice Shallow; he read a good deal, perhaps, but with "small Latin and less Greek" few of the standard classics —Ovid, Chapman's translation of Homer, North's of Plutarch; he became known to court folk but probably after he had written, not before; he did make a patron of the Earl of Southampton; he became a financial success in a bourgeois sort of way, but he never attended a council of state so far as we know, nor had he been in the tents of generals before and after battle; and his geography allowed him to speak of the seacoast of Bohemia. Perhaps the "dark lady" of the sonnets was a genuine person; she remains as nameless as the handsome young man to whom many of the sonnets were, almost amorously, addressed. He had seen plays, acted in them, patched them up, written them, no doubt done the job the modern "producer" does. We cannot check what Shakespeare wrote with his life, and yet very few have condemned what he wrote as being incredible. True, he made plays out of history, and historians have been showing his history wrong; it is our mistake, however, to take him to have been writing history when he could well have insisted he was only writing plays.

Suppose, then, as a stunt, that Shakespeare, sitting down to write *Henry IV*, thought something like this (let me modernize his language for I cannot imitate his): "I suppose I might as well fill in after Richard. I got Henry Bolingbroke on the throne in the Richard play, but he wasn't a very dramatic sort, a crowd-pleaser who thought everybody worked that way. There's nothing much in Holinshed to make a play of. The Northumberland rebellion wasn't much—badly treated by a suspicious king. They had Henry Percy, though, Hotspur. I could do something with him. He got killed, and by the young Prince Hal, the wastrel prince. That's the plot: the young, good-for-nothing prince reforms and kills the best warrior of his time! And Prince Hal later became the hero of Agincourt, which will give me another play the public ought to like. That old play I got hold of has Hal robbing tax collectors on Gadshill. We could make something of that, and joking in the tavern, but the public wouldn't want their prince really a criminal, so we'll have to keep him out of the robbery—amused by the robbers but not fooled by them. Those people at the tavern—we'll put them in. Who was that old knight in the play? Sir John Oldcastle! [The name Falstaff was not used in the first productions of the play.] Fat, on his uppers, but witty so the prince would really have fun with him. And then the battle of Shrewsbury, where Hal wins. We ought to have Oldcastle in the battle to tie the halves of the play together—pretending he'd killed Hotspur. That'll do—we'll have to rough in the rebellion somehow, and I suppose I'll have to play the king, so I ought to give him some lines, suspicious still, guilty, lecturing Hal, but a dismal man. Well, it's a beginning."

This is preposterous, of course, but no more impossible after all than most historical fiction. What would be experience here? Clearly several sorts: some of it bookish history, some of it national feeling, some of it personal acquaintance; but much of it theatrical experience, a feeling for the way a play must go, for what audiences will react to; and even a bit of personal buildup to give himself a part. From this outline, supposing one could have invented it, no one could foresee the whole detailed passage of the play. Not even Shakespeare could have foreseen what was going to come out as he set to the job of writing.

What came out came, we say, from his imagination. The human imagination is remarkable; perhaps the most we know about it is that it works on experience. The bowl-maker could not have imagined Persian or Greek stuff, as Einstein in 1000 B.C. or 1000 A.D. could not have imagined the theory his name now stands for. When we look at early and unskilled pieces of craft and sniff, "Well, I suppose they didn't know any better," we are not often aware that we are being literally true. They did not have the experience to imagine other ways of art.

We all have had experience of imagining things; we

have all had dreams. And some of us spend odd moments while brushing our teeth trying to check back the pieces of our dreams to recent actual experiences; sometimes we succeed, sometimes fail, but we hardly ever find a whole person or scene or speech in the dream just like its counterpart in real life. Imagination has been at work putting together in odd ways bits and pieces of old memories. The waking imagination works similarly; we do not know physiologically how. Some brains "imagine" more readily than others. We can make a few guesses that when the connections of the neurons work more easily and allow a stimulus to activate more and more brain cells, there is likely to be more imagination. Whatever the mechanics, things "pop" more quickly and more variously for some people than for others.

It is by imagination out of experience, out of stored memories to be made into new combinations, that artists chiefly work. Imagination can, in part, be forced by "taking thought," for thought is, after all, only imagination controlled by the really marvelous property, the will. Yet the process of thought will usually involve the massing of possibilities, analysis of them, rejection of most; and if you sat down to write a sonnet by "taking thought" throughout, you would find the process laborious and nearly a lifetime in length. You could not be sure you had the right adjective for the right noun until you had surveyed the possible adjectives, but, worse, you could not be sure you had the right "ideas" until you had surveyed the possible ideas, and out of all the possible ideas for sonnets how could you, by "taking thought," pick the "right" one? You would find ideas "popped" in thought as in imagination, but the process of analysis and rejection would discourage you, and you would finally let some "popped" idea ride as being good enough.

An artist simply does not have time to "think out" each detail of a complicated structure. Things "come to him." They come often so quickly and with so little effort of the will that the artist seems to himself to be "inspired."

The artist, then, must have had experiences, but it does not need extraordinary experience to make an extraordinary mind. What passion one has known will supply the nature of all passion. And, unless he be a hermit from infancy, he will have his society's ideas and attitudes, the reports of his fellows, and his own, even if minor, samples of "life." Imagination can carry on from there.

What the artist needs as much as imagination, however, is the ability for choice, either rejection or acceptance. Here, too, experience will count, of course, having accepted the bad and found out it was bad. Here artists need to have looked at other art, to associate with other artists, to find out possibilities, but also to find out what "works" and what does not work. Here artists need criticism, informal and formal. The growth of this ability to select becomes "taste," and taste is the great mark of character.

"Character," like the word "personality," is a very general word, but it implies a sort of organization, a something consistent and distinct. It will show in an artist's work; it is so that we can recognize artists in works we have never seen or heard and say, "That must be Beethoven!" or "Cole Porter!" All considerable artists, after they have grown to have taste, will show their characters. If we could date to any twenty-five years the pots found in one Indian pueblo, we could no doubt pick out the work of such a woman as the maker of the bowl heretofore shown. Indeed, the experts in Greek pottery feel reasonably assured what hands painted a good many of the pieces of Greek pottery found (there are thousands), even though they know few names and are reduced to inventing names like "the Achilles painter"—this one so-called because a famous sample pictured that hero.

Let me here put down two poems on the death of spring. The first is by Robert Herrick, a seventeenth-century Englishman:

Fair daffodils, we weep to see
You hast away so soon;
As yet the early rising sun
Has not attain'd his noon.
Stay, stay
Until the hasting day
Has run
But to the evensong;
And, having pray'd together, we
Will go with you along.

We have short time to stay, as you,
We have as short a spring;
As quick a growth to meet decay
As you, or anything.
We die
As your hours do, and dry
Away,
Like to the summer's rain;
Or as the pearls of morning's dew,
Ne'er to be found again.[1]

Herrick, who was a parson, could not look at the daffodils without also being overwhelmed by all his morality and his seventeenth-century feeling that nature was only a textbook for truths.

The other poem is by Onitsura, a Japanese poet of the eighteenth century. In Japanese it has the following shape:

Saku kara-ni
Miru kara-ni
Hano-no chiru kara-ni

Translated, through Harold Henderson,[2] it goes:

They blossom and then
We gaze and then
Blossoms fall and then—

Onitsura did not let his morality interfere with what he saw; he is reticent—the inscrutable Japanese, I suppose —but he picked this pair of incidents from spring, and as one supplies his own remembered feelings to those words, one is sure Onitsura felt the same. His reticence, though, and his generosity in letting you think your own thoughts are very different from Herrick's typically British insistence on telling you the point. The differences in craft idea about what a poem is, in social climate, and in personal character come out clearly, I think. Though both started from much the same sort of event, the results are different pieces of art.

In a given work personal character may come out as what we call "tone," a prevailing way of looking at things that carries throughout the work. Some artists seem always to have the same tone, but tone is a more partial word than character and more variable, work to work; the tones of Beethoven's "Third" and "Sixth" are different; the tones of *Macbeth* and *A Midsummer Night's Dream* are different, and both differ from the tone of *Troilus and Cressida.* Yet all three are recognizably Shakespearean in character, and perhaps, if you wish to push it, you could say that there *is* a general Shakespearean way of looking at things, which is the tone that underlies all he wrote.

A scherzo, however, is not a funeral march; one feels differently in listening to each; their *tone* is different though one man may have written both. So we can use words like gay and mournful about different pieces by the same man and still recognize the one character of the man in both.

Not many men have been as versatile and variable as Shakespeare. Most major artists have found it hard to be comic, romantic, tragic, all three. One of the marks of William Faulkner was his capacity to handle more than one type of thing, to change his tone while retaining his character. Most artists strike a "style" in technique and in the way of handling and relating subject matter, and their character maintains one tone everywhere. Indeed, it is by this sort of uniformity we chiefly recognize their work. And there are, of course, artists who seem to show very little character, whose work is indistinguishable from other men's work. Things made for machine reproduction tend to be so, not only because the machine must wipe out the individuality of the hand's stroke but because planning for machine fabrication usually means the simplification and regulation of factors. So the quality of a machine reproduction of a Persian carpet fails to equal that of a singly made original. Though one house of a "development" may have its character, and though houses are not yet fully made by machine, a whole development—at least as I have seen examples around many cities—will seem not only monotonous but finally without tone at all. Not only machine-made things lack character, however, for so do many individually made things, from gift-shop pots to Hollywood movies—though most movies are group-made and so their quality is diminished. "Styles" or "fashions" persuade designers to imitate, so that it takes something of an expert to pick out any individual maker of a "Queen Anne" chair. When there are few samples left of the fashions of the past, each alone returns to a character among things of its kind before and since. So each "antique" car in a rally of antique cars assumes a quality it had lost when there were dozens of it on the road.

The character of a good artist's work can almost never be captured by an imitator, for the imitator cannot duplicate the good artist's experience. It would be tedious if not impossible to show how individual experience comes out in individuality of character, yet the sample of work by imitators, such as the painter who some years ago put on the market several "newly found" Vermeers, will show the truth that character cannot be finally imitated; and the conclusion from that I take to be that the individual experience of the artist makes a difference of considerable import to the art.

The experience of the artist, then, is various, and what he makes of his personal past and his past and present imagination is his own, is, in a sense, "him." "He" will show, not because he expresses his opinion or because his work is extravagant and odd, but in the way he looks at things and makes us feel about them. Such a phrase as "the way he looks at things" is, again, very vague. I can suggest what I try to make the phrase mean by pointing out that we do not find Shakespeare alone in his language or Van Gogh, say, in his brushstrokes. We find Shakespeare also in our feeling about Falstaff and Hotspur and Cleopatra and Viola and Bottom the Weaver. Falstaff is not the jolly fat man whom we should all love and forgive, nor Prince Hal the noble and misunderstood young man filled with all the heroic virtues. We may wish that we could love Falstaff more; we may feel he deserves some sinecure at Hal's court at the end of *Henry IV*, Part

II. We may feel such a reformed hero as Hal would give him one—*noblesse oblige.* Then we may discover the real Shakespeare, harder, tougher, more thoughtful than we had taken him to be. We may discover a highly moral Shakespeare, whose judgment is less swayed by sentiment than we thought. And we may be able to put this Shakespearean clarity and sense of human principle together with that ability we have long recognized in him to make clear a variety of men and women. To make clear complexity and variety, to avoid the simple character serviceable for a play's action, to allow almost every actor a chance to make an effect on stage (remember the serving man who is made memorable simply by uttering "anon," a part a minor actor could take a little pride in performing)—these require a colder judgment than we think, and here we may find another Shakespeare than an all-commiserating one, a Shakespeare more intelligent than a romantic fashioner of phrases. And then we may examine some of the phrases and discover (here read William Empson's *Seven Types of Ambiguity*) the complexity of thought, even the exactitude of thought, that went into the phrases. It will teach us, of course, that it is harder to write a Shakespearean sonnet than we thought; it will also teach us that the Shakespeare who could have had relatively little experience of the court and of affairs of state had a capacity of imagination from what little he had experienced and a taste for choice that warrants all the plaudits of the years.

Perhaps I should put into this pot of words—experience, taste, character, tone—another word, "style." It is a word that refers, usually, more to the work itself than to the artist, but we do often use it in a very general way for a consistent quality, one manifest in the work, true, but one we throw back on the artist. When we say we can recognize this picture as one done by Rembrandt, we may say it has Rembrandt's style and point out his use of light and shade, his coloring, his brushstrokes, blurring of detail, surface finish, and such technical properties, but we may mean much more than this, something like character, a "way of looking at things." Yet I think I should prefer, in order to have one word mean one thing and not usurp the place of others, to let style refer only to technical qualities. After all, an artist may have distinctive character, poor taste, and vigorous style (Walt Whitman for one), and he may vary his tone from work to work, as Whitman could, even through a reasonably consistent style.

Let nothing said so far suggest that artists do not "work from life," for of course they do. The bison and horses and mammoths of the caveman were hardly done from animals who posed in the caves of Lascaux and Altamira, but the painters had made observations and were trying to reproduce life. And there have always been writers, I imagine, who were in considerable degree autobiographical. In our time and country Ernest Hemingway, for instance, seems to have been writing his own life, for many of the scenes he wrote can be related to what it has been discovered he did. He said himself, "Where we have been, you can go, too." There remains a doubt, however, that any scene is an exact reproduction, and "where we have been" includes the thoughts and feelings not only of his objective experience but of his later cogitation. "Hills Like White Elephants," perhaps his best story, was written, he said, in an afternoon in Paris after lunch with a girl he knew had had an abortion, though he did not discuss it with her. The biography of an artist may explain the sources of some of his ideas and may even be useful to discover ways of understanding the enigmatic, but the biography, though known in detail, could never be exactly related to the work—another tedious process even if one could complete it.

Nor do artists work entirely out of their own blue. They work, as I have kept suggesting, out of a tradition that says what a bowl should be, what a play should be. They also tend to work from previous subject matter: the Greek dramatists rifled legends; Shakespeare rifled history and Renaissance stories. Religious artists have a series of characteristics for their figures and stories: Buddha with his head bump, Peter with his keys, the Polynesian tiki with his off-center head on a mere blob of body. The confines of the given thing, like the confines of recognizable reality, force the artist to imagine within an area and so allow him to get some work done. Even fantasy such as that of Lewis Carroll depends upon known pieces of reality and is fascinating for its reversals of them. Inventions, experiments, the work of artists all need an object, a given, a subject to work up, as Shakespeare "worked up" Holinshed to *Henry IV*.

Nor is it likely that artists work without some catalytic experience to set their imaginations to work. Many work from necessity, of course, because they must produce to live. In the Renaissance days of general patronage, painters were commissioned to do a Madonna or a Holy Family—with patron kneeling, perhaps—and still today fortunate artists are so commissioned. Yet a sudden sight or meeting with people or even a sudden thought may be the seed of a piece of work. The potmaker may have seen someone else's pot, or she may have thought, "Let's divide the design up into threes"; the painter may have seen a view or a shape or a face or a combination of colors, or he may have been to an exhibition. The writer may have read a book or a newspaper or had cocktails with an actor or gone on a vacation or wandered through a city reclamation project or remembered something from his own past. The catalytic agent may be almost anything. A poet I recently talked with said a line "came to him," not a line of the kind he usually wrote, and he had to hunt around to find what it meant and what it might be related to, and hadn't yet managed to get a successful poem out of it.

The catalytic agent will often show, as in this story from out of those Franz Boas collected from the Kutenai Indians:

There was Coyote. All at once he saw Rabbit coming. He said to him: "Why are you running?" Rabbit said: "I am running away." He went past and went on. Coyote was sitting there. He thought: "Oh, something must have happened, and I might almost have been in trouble myself!" Coyote started to run. He went along and went along. There was a little prairie. There was Wolf. Wolf was there, and saw Coyote coming. Coyote arrived, and [Wolf said]: "Why are you running?" "I am running away." Coyote went past. Wolf was sitting there. He thought: "Oh, something must have happened, and I might almost have been in trouble myself!" Wolf started to run. He went along and went along. There was a little prairie. There was Grizzly Bear. He saw Wolf coming. When he was coming along and when he arrived he said to him: "Now, why are you running?" He was told: "I am running away." Wolf went past. Grizzly Bear stayed there, and thought: "Oh, something must have happened, and I might almost have been in trouble myself!" Grizzly Bear started to run. Grizzly Bear went along and went along. There was a prairie. There he saw the three friends. He went on, and arrived there. He saw Wolf sitting there, a little farther along Coyote, a little farther along Rabbit. Grizzly Bear said to Wolf: "Now, why did you run away? There is hardly anything to run away from." Wolf said: "I was staying there, and saw Coyote coming. When he arrived, I said to him, 'Now, why are you running?' He said to me, 'I am running away.'" Coyote was told: "And why did you run away?" He said: "I was staying there, and Rabbit came. When he arrived, I said to him, 'Now, why?' He said, 'I am running away.' I thought, 'Oh, something must have happened, and I myself might almost have been in trouble!' Then I ran away." Then Rabbit was told: "Now, why did you run away?" "I was eating branches, the wind was blowing, the snow fell from the trees, and a branch broke off the tree; it almost fell on me. Then it made me run away. That is what I meant when I said, 'I am running away.' " Then they laughed and separated. Now it is ended.[3]

It is pretty clear how this story started: the originator of the story, who probably was not the man who told it to Franz Boas, had seen the folly of his fellows following some baseless rumor. He took the traditional animal characters and arranged his little story. Yet here his taste shows: there is not an endless number of characters: the whole countryside does not come running, as a less restrained writer might have allowed to happen. And his craft experience let him keep the secret why Rabbit ran—and hence keep up our curiosity—until the end. Unlike Aesop, he let the story stand for its own moral.

The experience of the artist is various, then. It may be reflected fairly directly in his work, or it may appear as it does in Henry James, an artist who was always thinking of artistic methods but whose sense of being an outsider in European society, though he spent his life professing to be part of it, shows in almost everything he wrote. Personal, objective experience, however, is most often invisible, for it shapes itself into that consistent and indelible amalgam we call character.

Perhaps the most important experience of the artist is craft experience, which I have suggested was true of the Indian woman and of Shakespeare. Those who have not tried to make some sort of artistic thing are not likely to appreciate the amount of experience in the craft an artist needs. It is not alone experience in use of muscles or words or sounds, however, not experience in technical presentation alone—though you can tell a "pro" the moment he stands up to read for a part or to outline a picture or come up from the huddle to the scrimmage line. It is far more the experience of having made a piece of art; it is the Indian woman thinking of making a decorated bowl, of Shakespeare thinking of making a play. It is the knowledge of how good is good. As Browning sententiously but properly said, "The little more and how much it is, the little less and what worlds away." That difference, which may seem so slight, is not come by through taking thought, but only by practice, by experience, the experience of shaping your thought, your mind, your imagination to the creation of an artistic thing.

The young and the rebellious are often inclined to feel that craft experience is narrowing, a force that dulls imagination. We have had for fifty years now a number of breaks with old tradition by young, by old, by trained, by untrained. The general public's opinion of what a story or a picture or a piece of music is has been altered some, but it is a safe bet that fifty years from now much of the work of the iconoclasts will be forgotten. Dadaism and surrealism are dead; abstract painting and puzzle-writing like some of Franz Kafka are on the way out. Genuine innovators are, after all, rare, and all but a very few of them have been men filled with traditional craft experience, overfilled, perhaps, and imaginative enough to be sick of it. Most art, most great art is a development and refinement of something preceding. We do not know the wooden originals of Greek or Hindu temples; we do not know by what slow steps or what sudden jumps the wooden originals were fabricated. Who first invented bread? Is the widespread story of the flood an invention or the memory of actual experience? Darwin suggested slow changes; others have believed in more sudden jumps. In art both have occurred, no doubt, but the sudden jump demands for its accomplishment craft knowledge. Einstein had to have the mathematics to reach $E = MC^2$. Neither inexperienced hermits on the one hand nor such untrained craftsmen as explorers and members of the Foreign Legion on the other seem to have become great artists.

A mind comes out of experience, and out of a mind comes art. If now I have confused experience, man, artist, I think the confusion justified. It is popular to say, "He is a scoundrel, but he can write divinely." I am not sufficient scholar to pronounce that true or false down the ages. I should be inclined to doubt it, but an artist need not be great at something else to be a great artist, and his experience need show only in his art. If it be great art, he will have needed not so much great experience as great use of what experience he had.

CHAPTER 3

The Ordering of Experience

A PIECE of art is an organizing of experience, on both sides, that of maker and that of audience. As I have suggested, the desire to see an orderly thing and the desire to make one are almost instinctive in human kind, and though one can in Darwinian fashion explain the need for food, shelter, sex, and so on, one can less easily so explain the desire for order. It is true that it is only by order, by logic, if you prefer, that we can grasp the world at all; all words come from our success in relating and distinguishing things, from "putting them in order." A disorderly mind could probably not manage to survive in any primitive setting, and survives only by the help of others in a more civilized one. The cat stalking and catching the bird has an orderly way of activity that is an incipient drama. Purpose demands some sort of order, and few natural actions are quite purposeless.

In a sense, though, the order of art, like art itself, is purposeless. We must look, perhaps, another way here. What art does, of course, is to exercise the psyche. It stimulates and it completes, ends, finishes off, but we win no prize, catch no bird. This is something very few nonartificial experiences do and gives art the same distinction as gymnastics. The psyche is stimulated, stirred, satisfied. Such satisfaction can be most quickly seen in music, I suppose, where the completion of a motif or a phrase or a tune or even a simple scale becomes for the listener a psychic necessity. Somewhere I heard an anecdote, about Mozart I think, that one night after he had gone to bed someone downstairs played part of a piece on the piano but stopped before completing the final cadence. Mozart had to go downstairs and finish the cadence to the tonic triad before he could go to sleep. Not only a necessity, the psychic process is fun, a pleasure. Indeed, this may be what pleasure is, the stimulation and satisfaction of our minds. We used to be told that all we had was protective pain nerves, and that pleasure came from the end of pain, so that the old gag of beating your head against a wall because it feels so good when you stop was a paradigm. The doctors now, however, are finding pleasure centers in the brain, a positive means of pleasure rather than a negative one. At any rate, unless one wishes to regard the contented but inactive cow as the happiest thing in the world, or sleep as the best state, one must accept activity of some sort as pleasurable. Such activity art supplies and activity that seems to have a direction which drives it forward. Yet a mountain climber would not want, I think, an endless mountain; even the most pleasurable activity needs an end sometime, a surcease of tension. And it is conclusions, completions, that art supplies.

The most gripping, narrowing, absorbing of psychic stimulations and completions is probably the sexual. I was taught dramatic structure by a spinster lady who made us diagram plays under the headings of introduction, rising action, climax, falling action, conclusion. I suppose that in those pre-Freudian days the analogy did not cross her mind, as it did not cross ours. At any rate, we could, one way or another, make plays fit this structure. The major set pieces of Wagner are models of it—and of its sexual analogy. Let me, then, use it as a sort of extreme standard of the psychic process and suggest it as a way of our desire for order and for art. This is the way our psyches work.

It is, of course, a process in time, and we are accustomed to say that stories and plays and music and dance work in time but pictures and statues work in space. It is certainly true that the schemes of psychic response to a story and to a picture *are* very different. Nothing moves in a picture; though motion may be suggested, though figures may writhe and may loom, they are forever looming, as in this Japanese print of water (Figure 3). I think you can catch yourself feeling the water rise up and being a little surprised when you realize it has not collapsed. Not many pictures try to do this, however. If we wish to find the order in pictures we must look elsewhere: we must look at contrasts and likenesses. Artists and critics have used the word "tension" for such relationships almost as if there were a struggle between shape and shape, color and color, which portended some sort of victory of one. Such relationships are a little like the looming of the wave. There is, then, as we look at parts of a picture and then sense it as a whole, a kind of activity implied even in static relationship.

More motion than this sort, however, can be found within pictures and statues. Shapes like legs and arms seem to direct us here and there. With the discovery of the uses of the third dimension in European painting (Orientals knew it but did not use it fully in design), one's attention could be driven into a picture and, spi-

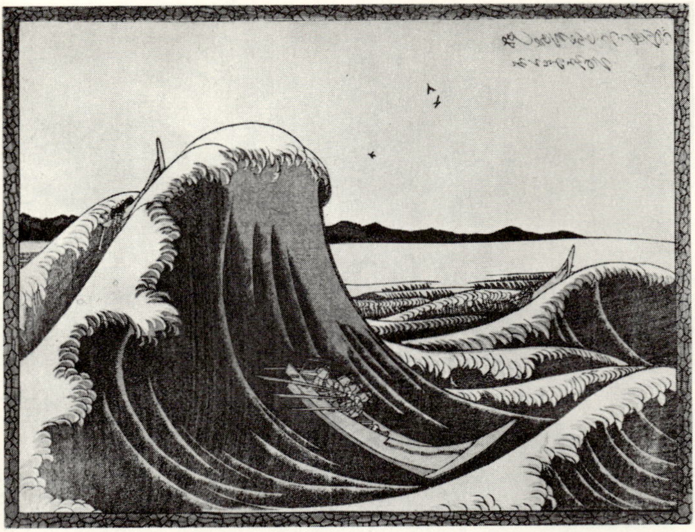

FIGURE 3. "Boat Being Carried by a Great Wave," Japanese wood-block print by Katsushika Hokusai. Courtesy of the Museum of Fine Arts, Boston

rally, around in it. Early sculpture had in most cultures only a two-dimensional design, with "motion" up and down or sideways. The Greeks, however, began to have feeling for the possible motions around a piece, for the coming forward and going back, for the spiral, and our latest sculptors make much play of going *through* a body or a shape. All such motions of our attention take place in time. They should not, of course, carry us out of the picture or out of the sculpture: they need either a kind of circle to travel or a place to stop and return from.

If we look at the famous reclining figure from the Parthenon (Figure 4), which used to be called Theseus and is now thought to be Dionysus or Ares, I think we will find our attention go up from the base to the supporting arm to the head, be directed by the direction of the face toward the broken right arm and so to the knees and back to the trunk; and perhaps we can go a shorter circuit around arms and head—perhaps the two hands once held a common object like a wand or thyrsos—which will in turn be balanced to our sight by the simpler motif of legs and lower trunk. If we look at this statue of the *Pietà* scene by Michelangelo (Figure 5), we may feel the motions upward in a sort of pyramid, stopped by the face of Michelangelo's sad self-portrait until our gaze is brought back down with his.

Such motions up and down, around, in and out cannot forever keep responses in a state of flutter or motion. I think we tend to move around a picture or a statue until we feel we know it, and then find, if it be a successful picture, the sense of its balance. Such balances may be very subtle, for the even contrast, the perfectly symmetrical—for instance a black square next to an equal white square—comes so quickly to balance that there is

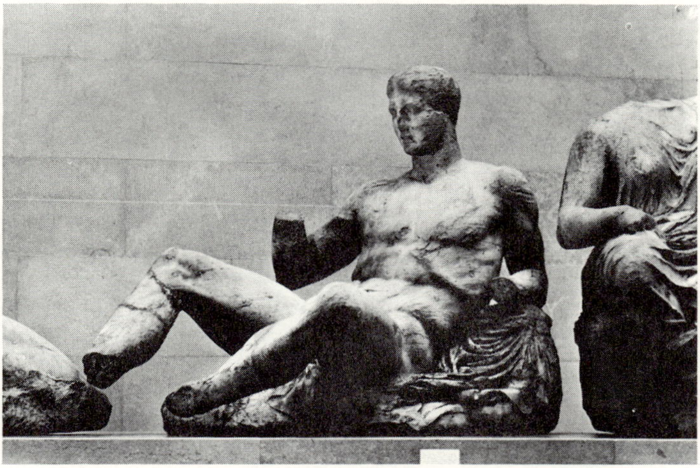

FIGURE 4. Figure from the Parthenon pediment, British Museum, London. Photograph by courtesy of Gjon Mili

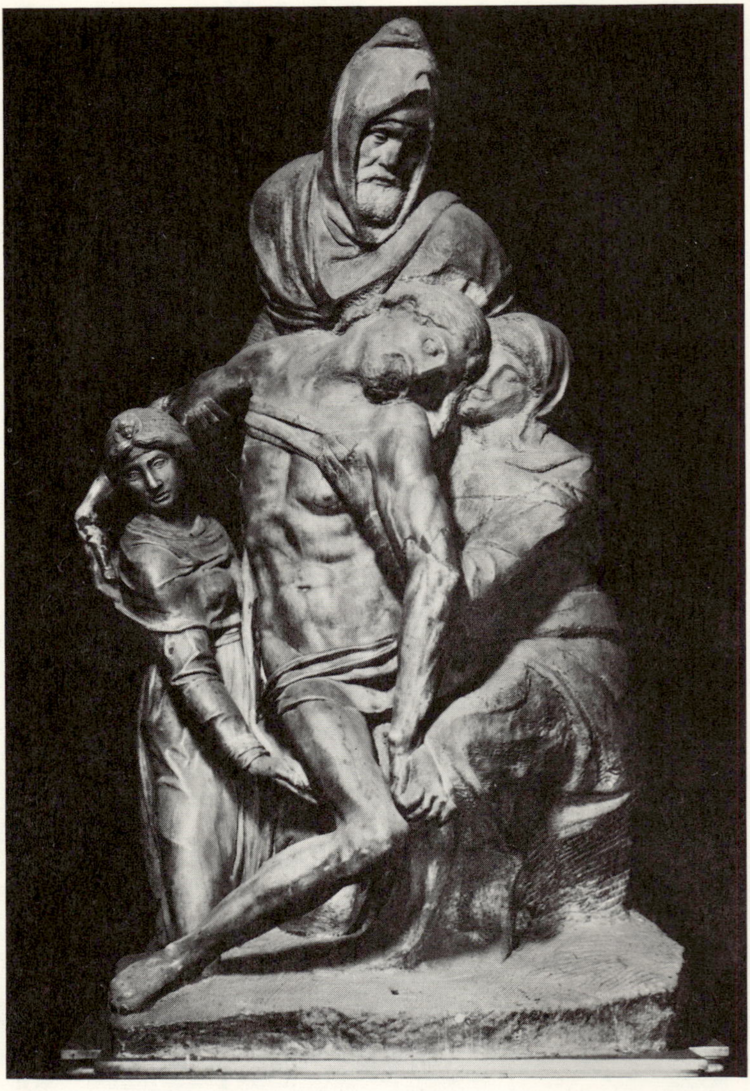

FIGURE 5. "Pietà" by Michelangelo, Duomo, Florence. Photograph by permission of Fratelli Alinari

no time for more than the briefest motion of the mind. Time of a certain sort, then, is involved in the satisfactory quality of static pieces of art, involved because some sort of as yet unseen or unreconciled relationship needs to start a question which time, great or small, can answer.

I think this is true of our responses to such things as portraits: we do not immediately sense the character, the person. We get suggestions from each of the features, one after another, sometimes from several almost simultaneously, until we feel we comprehend the whole. This is not a question of motions induced by shapes and directions, or of balances, but a question of the way the mind must comprehend. Thus we come back, I think, to an example, however short and slight, of the fundamental psychic stimulation and satisfaction.

A good many people have said that lyric poetry is like painting, a picture, a unitary feeling. I suppose the shortest and most pictorial of poetry is the Japanese haiku. Let me quote one in Harold Henderson's translation:

In the mountain village
Under the piled-up snow
The sound of water.[1]

The first organization of this we see may be the contrasts: stillness-motion, winter-chance of spring, silence-sound, white snow-black water, lack of life-people quiescent and waiting, the whole yin and yang contrast in which neither can be utterly victorious over the other.

Yet even here there is a kind of time sequence, for if we turn these phrases around—"the sound of water under the piled-up snow in the mountain village"—our minds fasten on the water right away and the rest is anticlimactic. As the poet wrote it, we have expectance: in, under—what?—ah, sound?—of water, the thing of vitality. However fast the syllables go, there is an infinitesimal space of question before answer here—if you like, a very small drama.

A great deal of lyric poetry depends for its basic structure on the grammar, the logic of a sentence.

When in disgrace with fortune and men's eyes
I all alone beweep my outcast state,
And trouble deaf heaven with my bootless cries,
And look upon myself, and curse my fate,
Wishing me like to one more rich in hope,
Featur'd like him, like him with friends possess'd,
Desiring this man's art, and that man's scope,
With what I most enjoy contented least;
Yet in these thoughts myself almost despising,
Haply I think on thee,—and then my state,
Like to the lark at break of day arising
From sullen earth, sings hymns at heaven's gate;
For thy sweet love remember'd such wealth brings
That then I scorn to change my state with kings.[2]

"When I feel badly, I think of you." I think one demands a resolution of the question set up: "And *then* how do you feel?" There could be alternatives: "I feel much worse" or "I feel better because I can't be as badly off as you"—and so on. Shakespeare answers the question quickly, of course: "and then my state,/Like to the lark at break of day arising. . . ." The grammatical or logical necessity of resolution has been met, and this order, I suspect, is what makes the poem effective. We could not reverse the order without dullness: "I feel good when I think of you when I'm feeling bad." There is a moment of hesitation, and a natural pause in reading, just after "Haply I think on thee." Thus there is time involved, and again a basic, if small, sample of the psychic curve of stimulation and satisfaction.

Perhaps the most famous of all statements about structure in literature is that of Aristotle speaking of tragic drama:

> Now a whole is that which has a beginning, a middle, and an end. A beginning is that which does not itself necessarily follow anything else, but which leads naturally to another event or development; an end is the opposite, that which itself naturally (either of necessity or most commonly) follows something else, but nothing else comes after it; and a middle is that which itself follows something else and is followed by another thing.[3]

This may seem an all too obvious statement, yet it covers a great deal, and it uses one series of words that all mean much the same thing but are definitive: necessarily, naturally, most commonly. No story can be interesting which does not pursue succession; succession must go on by "necessity." Necessity (what "naturally," that is, in an orderly way, happens) is the logic of time. There are philosophic objectors to necessity, for it seems to close down choice to human will; and scientists now and again confess all they can see is a statistical average of haphazard. Yet neither the philosophers nor the scientists accept a capricious world, and the choice is caprice or necessity.

Aristotle went on to use the word "consistency," a word closely allied but one which hints at things "seeming" to an observer. He goes on to say a probable impossibility is better to use in a play than an improbable possibility. Thus he shifts from objectivity to subjectivity, to the way things seem to the audience rather than the way they might be in objective nature. The disparity here is between the nature we cannot fully schematize and the logic of our minds; there should ideally be no disparity, and as we grow in knowledge there comes to be less and less; but Aristotle plunks for our logic as against what we do not know of nature's.

These ideas may seem some distance from the curve of psychic response, but they are the substance of the means to satisfaction. It is not hard for an artist to stimulate us, to draw our interest; it is much harder for him to answer, to reach solution, to balance factors. The means to that derive from a rigorous following of the logics of succession. If we examine one of Molière's most famous plays, *Tartuffe,* we will see that Molière had written himself into a jam; his villainous, false cleric, Tartuffe, has so much more intelligence than the dupe, Orgon, that Orgon and his family cannot be saved by any of those on the stage so far; yet he must be saved or vice will triumph, and Molière's play will be a propaganda play pure and simple and the audience of his time no doubt outraged. Molière invented, to save Orgon, a hitherto unheard-of criminal record for Tartuffe and the all-seeing eye of the king: the unexpected marines arrive in time, so to speak. It is a possible conclusion, but neither logical nor probable, and it is not a satisfactory one. It is, I think, a defect in an elsewhere great play; yet Aristophanes had similar trouble, and so had Shaw and Congreve and Jonson, for the author who wishes to show the folly of stupidity must often show the intelligence of vice, a contest in which logic finds a "happy ending" hard to come by.

More sober writers find similar troubles: Dostoevsky purges Raskolnikov suddenly at the end of *Crime and Punishment* and has Dmitri escape in *The Brothers Karamazov,* but in these books the wind has gone, Aristotle's end been reached before these scenes, so that logic this late does not matter.

The artist's problem of logic is to battle the sentiment

of the audience, even his own sentiment as his own audience. Let me illustrate the uses of logic in two poems. The first one is a difficult poem:

I saw a chapel all of gold
That none did dare to enter in,
And many weeping stood without,
Weeping, mourning, worshipping;

I saw a serpent rise between
The white pillars of the door,
And he forc'd and forc'd and forc'd;
Down the golden hinges tore,

And along the pavement sweet,
Set with pearls and rubies bright,
All his shining length he drew
Till upon the altar white

Vomiting his poison out
On the Bread and on the Wine,
So I turned into a sty
And laid me down among the swine.[4]

This poem of William Blake's brings up very clear pictures, I think: the chapel, the people, the snake forcing his way in, going down the nave, pouring poison on the altar, and "I" of the poem turning to the swine. And I think all these images come with strong feelings attached to them. The chapel of gold seems a good thing. By and large, people left out in the cold and waiting to get in bring out our democratic and underdog sympathies. Most of us don't like snakes, and the violent use of power by something we don't like offends us. As I think of this poem from time to time, I am never sure whether the serpent draws his *shining* length or his *slimy* length; somehow his going along the floor of gems seems horrid. Although I am not personally attached to them, altar, bread, wine seem valuable, sacred, and the vile sounds of the words vomiting and poison are disgusting. We have a series of pretty strong attitudes so far, and we can feel the dramatic situation; we don't know why "I" turns away to the pigsty instead of, say, killing the snake, but we sense a revulsion so strong that the companionship of pigs, not on the face of it good company, is better.

One can get most of the experience of the poem, its pictures and their attendant feelings; one can feel the order of the poem, question, action, reply, both without having the slightest idea what the poem is about: what chapel? what people? what snake? why turn to the pigsty? It has order, an internal logic of events, and an internal logic of feeling. It is almost, since one doesn't understand its external meaning, an abstract poem, one less jocular than, say, "Jabberwocky."

One feels, of course, it has some external meaning, symbolically expressed. What chapel?—what snake? The sexual symbolists, calling themselves Freudian, will immediately clamor that this is a rape scene, and "I" decides, if love can be so desecrated, he might as well become low as the beasts himself. Though this interpretation may add to the revulsion, it does not explain chapel and mourners outside, and Blake would hardly have made sexual symbols of sacred ones.

Blake, of course, was opposed to the whole Establishment in England, as various poems will show, this bit among others:

> *God and his Priest and History,*
> *Who make up a heaven of our misery.*[5]

But the people were not really *outside* the Church in England, nor would the rapacious clerics and lords have been likely to desecrate the symbols of wealth, gold and jewels; *quite* the opposite.

We must examine the snake again. What snakes do we know? The most famous came in the Garden of Eden. And what was the burden of his argument? Knowledge, reason—as against innocence and faith. Looking at others of Blake's poems—"Mock on, mock on, Voltaire, Rousseau"—we will find Blake scorning the rationalism of his time. Perhaps this snake is eighteenth-century rationalism.

The chapel cannot be the Garden of Eden, however, where inside were Adam and Eve and outside was nobody yet. Blake writes frequently, though, of a return to, a reconstitution of, what he called the New Jerusalem, an age of innocence, of simple faith, where lion and lamb and pig can lie down together. The chapel, then, may be that Kingdom of Love to come in which men have faith, and the pig its humblest, most outcast, and most unreasoning symbol.

I cannot assure you this is the proper reading of the poem, for those who have written about Blake have treated this poem most gingerly, but if I am right, it says: The people mourn for their heritage, the New Jerusalem, but the snake of Reason desecrates it, and I turn away from reasoning man to innocent animals. The "I" of the poem is no hero who slays the "frumious Bandersnatch" of "Jabberwocky" but a man who retreats. The story, then, the destruction of Faith by Reason and retirement, is parallel to the emotions generated by the pictures themselves: the emotional order and the intellectual order are one.

You may disapprove Blake's position, be on the side of Reason against Faith, but you cannot deny Blake's truth, that Reason has tended to destroy the innocence of Faith.

It is, I think, a logical poem, internally and externally.

The other poem is one by Walt Whitman:

When I heard the learn'd astronomer;
When the proofs, the figures were ranged in
columns before me;
When I was shown the charts and the diagrams, to
add, divide, and measure them;
When I, sitting, heard the astronomer, where he
lectured with much applause
in the lecture-room,
How soon, unaccountable, I became tired and sick;
Till rising and gliding out, I wander'd off by
myself,
In the mystical moist night-air, and from time to
time,
Look'd up in perfect silence at the stars.[6]

This poem has a kind of order: when I heard the astronomer—what?—I felt sick and went out—what for?—to look at the stars. It is a logical sentence. And it has an emotional expansion from being shut up inside to the larger outside and the conclusive look upward at the stars. It is based on much the same general motif as Blake's poem is: that Reason, here scientific, destroys something sacred, one's wonder at the stars.

The order, however, is different. Blake's poem goes:

There's a good chapel
The snake desecrates it
And I turn away.

As you go along, your emotional questions are answered and you feel the order. Whitman's poem goes:

The astronomer lectures
I leave
and go look at the stars.

Whitman forces you to check back at the end to account for what he calls "unaccountable," his disgust with the astronomer. After all, we have all heard long lectures, and in general, I imagine, are not very violently antipathetic; why should the astronomer have so excited Whitman? Thus, we do not follow his emotional logic during the poem. He forces us to check back, and when we check back, I think we reach an area of dispute: does the astronomer desecrate the stars? I think my sense of wonder, my awe, is increased by the astronomical knowledge I have, little as it is. Thus, one can dispute the external logic of Whitman's poem. Had he put the order of his poem:

The stars are sacred
The astronomer desecrated them
I sicken and leave

he would have had Blake's order and emotional logic. You could then have asked, "Isn't he entitled to his opinion as much as Blake was?" Even then I am afraid I must answer "No," for Blake's thesis, that Reason destroys Faith, seems true, while Whitman's, that the astronomer destroys our wonder at the stars, does not.

This has been a very long illustration of the place of logic, internal, emotional, external, in what we can call artistic order. I hope that it shows that an emotional man of faith like Blake can—and must—"think" well artistically, that emotional order demands intellectual order even to be emotionally effective. My response to Whitman, though I have no doubt he believed and felt as he wrote, can be elegantly phrased only by some such word as "rubbish."

In the story, we have had over time several major orders. The first kind of story, I suppose, was about "what happened." The opening situation—"once upon a time there was—" led to an event which produced another event, and another, and these then came to an outcome—end of story. This is the "tale," which you will find in various forms in Boccaccio and Chaucer in the European tradition. This might be a mere series of odd events, or it might have something like a "dramatic" structure, and so come to a decisive moment in which you can foresee alternatives: one man or the other wins in the battle. This is the buildup of suspense, one of the tensions of uncertainty in the process of the psychic curve. Oddly, though we may rationally be sure which man will win, we can still be mechanically aroused, for the psychic curve from question through uncertainty to resolution may work almost in the fashion of a conditioned reflex.

The second kind of story comes out of this: the moral story, in which one man is "good." We are led to be on his side; we "sympathize" with him, for his character or for his goals, and often we "hate" his opponent. In the first story our emotional involvement is neglected for the mere fascination of events to conclusion. The second story draws on our feeling for "good" people as against "bad" ones. We are not for or against Oedipus or Hippolytus or Achilles; indeed, Hector, whose humanity may win us to the neglect of his foolish pride, is for many readers of the *Iliad* a sentimental favorite. But Samson has to be justified, even in his blindness he must do some heroic deed; and Joseph has to be a success, having been the "good" guy against his brothers. Our involvement in the moral story through our affections for people we like is the guiding motif of the second kind of story. Here, still, events and their logical succession count, and the saving of the good not by logic but by extraordinary accident—one of the most well-known examples appears in

Hardy's *The Return of the Native* in the final dice game —makes us a little unhappy in our happiness. Life often lets the bad guy win, especially when we have bet against him, but the story of the second, moral kind must arrange our emotional satisfaction.

Since the time of Chekhov in European literature, however, the story of events has given way to the story of theme or feeling. Here events happen, of course, but their causal relation is neglected, and they do not come to a foreseen climax of suspense. The psychic curve is of a different kind. In Chekhov's "The Student," for instance, a young student priest comes on a cool spring night to the fire of some peasant women; he tells them the story of Peter in the garden—it is the night before Easter—and finds through their tears at the story that life is linked and alike down the ages; he feels very happy, a "part of it all." There has been no succession of events in the old sense; nothing "happens." Chekhov could have left the story here, and we would say, "Ah, a *theme* story!" He puts in, however, a few excessive words about the young man's happiness and adds "he was only twenty-two"; the theme is undercut, and what we feel, I think, is the older man, Chekhov, and ourselves judging the perhaps sentimental enthusiasm of youth. If one does not expect suspense and "outcome," one reads this story, I find, with a kind of delight and comprehension. We are teased into a "great truth" and then shocked out of it by Chekhov's last sentence. We have been through an experience to a conclusion.

Joyce in *Dubliners* and Hemingway in *In Our Time* made this sort of story popular. It is a kind of story whose dynamism may seem more poetic than narrative, yet it is normally less dependent on grammatical logic than the poem is; it is a building of feelings and attitudes whose constructive logic is not easy to explain and, I am sure, not easy to create. It has the danger of becoming a sort of intellectual observation—ah, yes, young men are like that! Yet it can, as Hemingway manages in "Hills Like White Elephants," bring a sudden "illumination" about things—in that story, about the gap between taking life honestly and trying to outwit it.

I have already suggested that there may be more than one order to a piece of art: some form of time sequence, a question and answer, a grammatical logic, a succession of feelings, and a possible external logic, one that at least convinces us, a "probability." In such a story as Faulkner's "Dry September" several forms of order are at work, but some seem incomplete. The story is based on a lynching. It comes in five sections. There is an opening paragraph or two in which the terrible psychological effect of drought is suggested; then we find in a barber shop the rumor that a white woman has been raped, the white men whipped up by an ex-soldier named Plunkett, the barber trying to be reasonable and trying—you feel ineffectually—to stop their going after a Negro named Will Mayes. The second scene shows the past of the white woman, a lady who had not managed to get married. The third scene takes us in a car with the men who have caught Will Mayes; the barber, who is along, is ineffective; we are where Mayes will be killed, but we are not shown the killing, only the escape of the barber from complicity. The fourth scene shows us the white woman having hysterics at the movies and her friends wondering if anything did happen at all. The final scene shows Plunkett coming home, being brutal to his wife, and sweating out on his porch under the continuing heat, internal and external. It is, then, a story not exactly about a lynching, for the lynching itself goes on offstage; not exactly about a rumor, for we are never told outright that the story of the rape was made up; not exactly about the psyche of the lynchers, for they talk but are hardly analyzed; not exactly about Plunkett, though it is on him our eyes rest at the end; nor is it a story of the evil effects of a bad climate, though that is the suggestion of its title; nor is it a propaganda piece about injustice exactly, for at the end we don't want to do anything; our hatred somehow dies. These possible orders involve us but do not conclude and so satisfy us. Yet the story is powerful; we go through fear, hatred, disgust, a sense of doom, to a final revulsion, cut off by a last sentence that puts us under the "lifeless and indifferent stars," a cosmic frame. The dominant order, then, seems at first the generation of our revulsion, our "ugh!" complete and, because we neither want to do anything nor can, satisfied. A little later we may find that our revulsion dies, and what we are left with is a comprehension of the whole situation: we understand it. And this kind of order, from questions out of incomprehension to answers *and* comprehension, may be as effective on our feelings and our satisfactions as on our more intellectual responses. It is the major order in portraits.

Order, then, is not the simple thing of the diagram my spinster teacher taught me. Yet there must be order, some question, some expectation, some completion, as in the most famous of our recent antirealist plays, *Waiting for Godot,* we are presented by the first words, "Nothing to be done," a question—about what?—and find through the succeeding, seemingly inconsequent speeches and actions what nothing is to be done about and why.

I have perhaps overstressed so far the theory that time must be at work in artistic order. It is possible to say that after a story or a play or a picture or a piece of music one no longer feels succession but a kind of unity; things have lost their linear quality and have become a globe, a gestalt, a picture, a summary and inclusive feeling. It would be possible to say that the artist uses order to generate this postexperience gestalt. Yet I wonder. J. D. Salinger's often anthologized story "Uncle Wiggily in Connecticut" brings one ex-Vassar girl to visit another; they drink and talk an afternoon away; the talk is interesting but seems purposeless and ultimately drunken; yet at the end when one says about her now long past, "I was a good girl, wasn't I?" one senses suddenly the gap of tragedy between past and present; the whole comes into shape, into a sequence, as it does when the detective in a murder mystery sits down and explains what happened for the characters and for you, the reader. The thing finally "jells," we say, but jells, often at any rate, into a time sequence.

Whether in a time sequence or not, however, the "jelling" is the important thing; what has been uncertain, unanswered, is now answered, the psychic curve is complete, and we are satisfied. If we feel at the end the parts fit, as we get the parts to fit in a picture puzzle—an operation often of very considerable time—the artist has created order. Whether this is by the logic of time or by the logic of balance in space is less important than that it occurs. The very long novel *The Brothers Karamazov* is based on a few simple questions: will Dmitri kill his father? did Dmitri kill his father? will he get off? There is a great deal that seems irrelevant to these questions; we cannot explain their relevance, I suspect, but when we are through we somehow feel they were all relevant except for one passage, Alyosha's dealing with a precocious boy named Kolya. Then we learn from Dostoevsky's biography that he intended a sequel. I am glad he did not write the sequel; I would not feel art were being desecrated by an editor who cut the Kolya passages out of the novel as it stands.

The artist turns his experience into order. He can almost never do this in his head before he starts to work; what he puts down first will change what he thought he had in mind and will change his organizing scheme, perhaps. C. Day Lewis said that a poet might not know what his poem was to be about but found out as he went along writing it. Order, then, is seldom something fully imposed on experience; it is more proper to say, perhaps, order is wrought out of experience by the very process of ordering it. Shakespeare, one supposes, did not foresee that he would give Falstaff so much of *Henry IV* as he did; he had never given his clowns that much space in a "history" before and would not again. He let Falstaff run away with the play; no star who performs in the play plays any part but Falstaff. It may have been a "dramatic" mistake; I am glad he let it happen.

I have described order as it has come out in the finished product. It would be nice to be able to discuss it as the artist created it, yet few artists have left testimony of the process of their creation. There are, it is true, work sheets various poets have left that show the alterations made, and there are various sketches painters made before they made the final picture. These tell something; they do not show the opening purpose, or many of the reasons for change, or the trials and rejections never set down at all. And probably no artist could ever remember —or be much interested in remembering—the whole process he went through. We must speak of order, then, as it has come out, and as it affects us, for we have little way of knowing what the artist hoped it would do.

The process of creation is largely the process of arranging, of ordering. We know it by its product, the created thing.

CHAPTER 4

Self-sufficiency

PERHAPS there will be little argument about experience and order; about "self-sufficiency" there may be more. After all, we can say about art that it is a revelation of man to man and perhaps the most effective we have had so far. We can say that art teaches something.

We can say, as I shall try to show in a later chapter, that art is moral in the broadest sort of meaning of that term. There is no gainsaying the religious purposes of much of the art of history: that it was meant to celebrate divinity, that it was meant to inspire devotional feelings, that it was meant to protect—lares, house herms, fetishes, amulets—and that it was meant, as a magic influence, to secure fertility. The more artistic the object, the greater its power perhaps, though some very old and crude objects maintained greater power than newer and fancier ones, as the ancient statue of Athena made from a log of wood and supposedly fallen from heaven was the most powerful effigy of all to the Athenian mind. Yet the "more artistic" is a different phrase from the "more religious" and means something different, and it is the first that we are after discovering.

The nub of the controversy lies, I think, in whether the artist uses his experience to shape his art or uses his art to express his experience. Suppose two people are looking at a portrait. One says, "That's just like him!" The other says, "Well, not the way I saw him." There enters a third person who says, "I never knew the man, but it's a darned fine picture." It would be hard here to find what were the painter's motives: he had been commissioned and paid to do a "likeness"; he had studied the man and had a view of the character he wished to show; he had worked pretty hard to place, light, model, relate the parts of the head and bust into a thing of order. Viewer number one saw the first motive, viewer number two the second ("not the way I saw him"), and viewer number three the third. Would you say that the third man was the one who saw the portrait artistically?

There has, of course, been a long argument about representation, "mimesis," holding the mirror up to nature. In our tradition, Plato was perhaps the first to phrase it: he regarded a picture as a copy of an appearance (the thing pictured) that was itself only a mortal and changing example of the immortal and "real" form or idea. Painting was for him, then, secondhand imitation and nothing more, and his sentiments about literature derived from the same insensitivity. Aristotle, his pupil, used the word mimesis, too; but, plainly more acquainted with art than Plato, he seems to have regarded mimesis as representation not of the thing as is, but as it generally is, so that his painter would be rendering Plato's ideal reality. What Shakespeare meant by his "mirror up to nature" is very hard to tell; against the extravagances of some of his contemporaries he "rings true," but that kings or clowns ever actually talked as his do I doubt that he would insist.

An artist may indeed intend representation. He cannot,

naturally, make the thing he imitates: the portrait is not the man, or the funeral march men marching at a funeral. Nor can he give all. The story of what a man does and thinks of and feels during one day of his life would take millions of words, and a reader would gag after the first fifteen minutes of the day. The Chinese have pretended to draw each leaf on a tree, but I fancy a count would show any full tree's actual number reduced to a tenth or less by the artist. Once painters made a great number of strokes for the hair it was traditional to hide, and not quite hide, Mary Magdalene's body in, but the hairs on her head were too many for any painter to imitate, and later painters found a brushstroke would summarize a thousand hairs. The brushstroke would give the effect, the "impression," as our eyes indeed summarize for us by their focus.

The artist, then, must find summary symbols, must select, must "fake," just as the scientist does when he talks about "an" electron. His intention may still be to show the thing. It is true, I believe, that parts of cities have been rebuilt after war by examining old pictures, and anyone who has compared a Canaletto painting with present-day Venice will discover the painter's accuracy and be able to pick out the changes made in two hundred years. My wife and I have in our living room a print given to her of what we call "a piece of sod" by Dürer: grasses, flowers, weeds, and a pool. It has no lighting and thus does not give a visual "impression"; nothing is blurred, and the whole is, of course, "arranged," but no more than a photographer might manage. There the grasses are—not pretty, not significant, not made to suggest the "handiwork of God," not judged, but simply selected and presented by Dürer, who can be imagined as saying, "See!" I don't think the picture makes my mind go out to grasses I've seen, or in the winter nostalgically remember the joy of summer, or think of the ever renewing fertility of the earth. I remain within the picture, and I find it satisfying, as I find Canaletto's Venetian pictures satisfying. Wordsworth seems to scorn his character Peter Bell, saying of him: "A primrose by a river's brim a yellow primrose was to him." I am not sure that Peter Bell was not more artistic than Wordsworth, who wanted him to use the primrose for some truth or emotion or other. Gertrude Stein's famous "A rose is a rose is a rose is a rose" rebels against all the "false compare" of roses. If you look at a field and some trees with the naked eye, the factors tend to blur; you will overlook details, cannot focus on them, because of the limit of resolution of the eye. If now you look through a pair of binoculars, details will suddenly leap into sight: grasses, wild flowers, leaves, branches will seem to have a new life. You will have a "revelation," a shifting of your old conception and a startled moment until you resolve into the new. In a little way I find this "moving." Dürer's "Grasses" and Canaletto's Venice pictures do this for me, show me the "thing" more clearly than I would have seen it.

Yet even presentation must be colored by the character of the artist, as Dürer's grasses were. One of the early little scenes Hemingway published was an incident told him by a photographer and may retain some of the photographer's style of separate "clicks":

> They shot the six cabinet ministers at half past six in the morning against the wall of a hospital. There were pools of water in the courtyard. It rained hard. All the shutters of the hospital were nailed shut. One of the ministers was sick with typhoid. Two soldiers carried him downstairs and out into the rain. They tried to hold him up against the wall. Finally the officer told the soldiers it was no good trying to make him stand up. When they

fired the first volley he was sitting down in the water with his head on his knees.[1]

Hemingway was still a reporter trying to be an author when he wrote this. It is almost completely "objective," most of it visual. It comes out pretty clearly. The details are few, separate "shots" of vision, selected. At first it may seem simply a scene, an incident, but it will soon become more than that. It becomes sordid, unfeeling, "inhuman," horrible in some degree, even in and of itself, even if you don't put it up against the sentimental standards of glory and sacrifice and dignity in war. Hemingway, who had seen a good deal by then, picked this incident, shaped it, presented it. I think one cannot avoid feeling him behind it, the rebellious but sensitive Puritan from Illinois. The fact refuses to remain fact, representation to remain merely mimetic, in Hemingway's hands—or in ours.

This pair of shoes by Van Gogh was, I think, his attempt to get down these shoes as honestly as he could (Figure 6). His line and his brushstrokes have a personal character, of course, and he, like Dürer, uses no realist, shadow-casting light, so that the impression is not altogether visual. Yet I feel he was trying to do "shoes," and that these are shoes is immediately apparent. Is this all? Plato said if you wanted to find out about shoes, you'd go to a cobbler, but maybe Van Gogh tells you something the cobbler couldn't. It seems to me that here the shoes, because they are distorted by wear and could never have been very elegant, suggest a wearer, a poor and hardworking wearer, so that, in a sense, they become symbols of laboring humanity. Even if we happen to know they were Van Gogh's own shoes, their symbolic quality remains, I think. Whatever Van

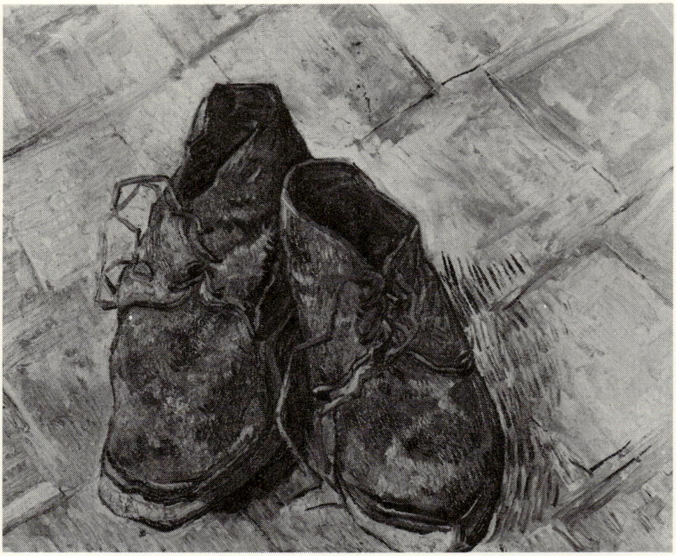

FIGURE 6. "Shoes on a Tile Floor," oil painting by Vincent van Gogh. Courtesy of Mrs. Siegfried Kramarsky

Gogh "meant" by them, our own fancy decorates them, and for us, if not for the artist, the fact again refuses to remain the fact.

So the little haiku I quoted before,

In the mountain village
Under the piled-up snow
The sound of water,

refuses to be just picture and becomes symbol for yin and yang, or, though the Japanese might not think this way, of life and death, neither ever finally dominant.

Dürer's "Grasses" do not send me very far from themselves; Hemingway evokes more than the scene itself from me, a judgment; and Van Gogh more, of a somewhat different sort. All of these, perhaps, intended a mirror. I doubt, however, that it was a purely visual mirror they intended. Hemingway said he wanted to give you "the way it was." This is not as clear a term as it seems, for "the way" may mean more "feel," more subjectivity, than objectivity, and whose subjectivity can be expressed but the artist's? The artist may wish for the "essence" of things; I think Van Gogh had good enough eyesight to know that his picture was no photograph; I suspect what he wanted was the "shoesiness" of shoes. Once started on subjectivity, one finds it hard to define a stopping place. Indeed, things that seem to represent no actual things may represent a state of mind, as the paintings of Soulages, made of black bars across brightness, may suggest an inability to "get through" to friends or family. Furthermore, perhaps no artist wants to let his audience overlook his art. This may be pride; it may be, too, his feeling that he can speak as writer, painter, musician only *by* his art, not in the discursive, external language of the philosopher. The news photographer may want his audience to go through his photograph to the man he pictured, the president, say, may want his audience to feel in the presence of the president. The news reporter may feel likewise, but what Hemingway was doing between his career reporting the external news and his career as a writer of fiction was trying to find a language and an order that stopped us at his words, put a distance between us, the readers, and the scene described, and in that space let us grow that comprehension of the scene's implications which he wanted us to feel. He could do that only by some form of selection, isolation, and consistency.

Reality is, of course, complex, confusing, and hard to organize. The cinema most clearly shows the difficulty of reality, for the camera is faithful: it is hard to see a movie of a good-looking girl walking through a dump as a symbol of anything, for both girl and dump are visually too real, too complex; for many viewers the girl will not register as beauty in an ugly civilization, only as a good-looking girl walking through a dump. The movies that have tried to be visually suggestive—beyond those which show handsome scenery for its own sake—have blurred focus, have exaggerated contrasts of black and white, have taken shots from odd positions which have enlarged or diminished the size of things or have skewed viewpoints, have concentrated on faces or hands or feet, and so on, at every moment trying to defeat reality, to point and isolate and simplify.

The same attempt is true of plays and stories. The realist drama with its persuasions of real setting, its likely costumes, its natural tones of voice and gesture is like the news photo of a president. Recent drama has tried to escape the complexity of the real by often extravagant simplifications and exaggerations of characters and of their costumes and makeup. When Samuel Beckett wished to enliven the texture of his basically dismal *Waiting for Godot,* he used the old tricks of the French circus, like those of our burlesque, which go back in time through Molière and the Commedia dell'Arte to the street plays of Rome and Athens and have their parallels in the comic antics of tribal peoples all over the world. Though George Bernard Shaw was working in a realist time, the liveliness of his stage and its significance are due to his judicious simplifying and stylizing of his characters; and Shakespeare, however Dr. Johnson talked of his "naturalness" and however complex his language, kept his characters intense and simple and exaggerated.

A strange result appears here: the monster Caliban and the fairy Ariel seem quite as vital, as full of "being," as Prospero and Miranda. Surely no one can deny the vitality of the Mad Hatter and the Red Queen and the Caterpillar in Lewis Carroll's fantasy, nor for millions of children and grown-ups the personal and living presence of Piglet and Eeyore and Winnie the Pooh. The issues among which Clytemnestra and Macbeth and Tartuffe move may seem of more concern to grown-ups than the issues of Alice and Piglet and even of Eliza Doolittle, but the vitality and fictional presence are the same, and achieved by the same simplification and the same falsity.

The phenomenon of falsity, then, is not so much phenomenal as necessary if we are to be kept back from losing ourselves in the complexity of reality and are to be, contrariwise, persuaded to see the problems, motions, issues, resolutions of the art before us. Without this "distance" between art and viewer our response might well be limited, uncertain, and unprofitable, for we do not know what to make of, how to react to unorganized, unsimplified reality. Thus, though we may see Hemingway's little scene as "real," we may realize how simplified it is, how carefully each of its few details—"the shutters . . . were *nailed* shut"—steers us and unifies our response. Hemingway didn't want it to be just a scene, and he tried not to let us let it be just that. If he wished to impress us, he could not have written otherwise.

The tendency of some of the art of recent times toward simplification, abstraction, nonrepresentation has been to find a purity of evocation, a stimulus nonassociative and hence nonsentimental. Even the musicians, whose notes might be thought pure enough, have tended to avoid the possible emotional appeal of melodies and themes and of tempos that one could dance to. No one seems to dance or even sing to the more advanced developments from "jazz." The struggle toward pure musical sound—or toward sound, musical or not—and the struggle toward pure color and shape, and the struggle in dance toward pure movement of a geometric kind have produced things of interest and sometimes of intensity, but I find the intensity short in duration and finally barren. The neglect of more evocation than the mechanical stimulation of eye and ear reduces art to the status of the Pueblo bowl. This is satisfactory for a bowl, perhaps, but it misses almost the whole range of our remembered feelings which art, and especially literature, can tap. Falsity can go too far, "distance" can become too great.

Does the calling out of our remembrances, the creation of new feelings toward real things, the allowing us to take Van Gogh's shoes for symbols of laboring humanity, for instance, turn us outward toward the world, or does the art use these for itself? Is the picture "a darned fine picture," or is the man pictured "a darned fine man"? Are you willing to be stirred and resolved for the sake of stirring and resolution or only for the product useful for life? There is no arbiter to decide this controversy, only one's own choice of a way to regard art.

There are, of course, artists who unmistakably wish to comment on life and society and so make their art valuable as document for the outer world. I suppose, though I have not counted, that such commentators are chiefly comedians. This has been traditional, perhaps, for the comedies of Athens, unlike the tragedies, dealt with contemporary life and seemed worthy of consideration only if seriously concerned about the life they made funny. More than tradition, however, makes it almost inevitable that anything beyond buffoonery, if it wishes to be funny, must be funny "at the expense" of someone's folly, and the joke will draw audience feeling more strongly, I suppose, if the character be not odd but a common type. The clown is a clown and not like people we know, but the pompous, the pretentious, the garrulous are members of our society. If, then, they be given a general social habit to be foolish about, the result will be social comment, almost willy-nilly.

Even if commentary were not inescapable, comic writers from Aristophanes down have used comedy as a deliberate political and social weapon. And not comic writers alone, of course; there has been art of comment and protest that has not been comic at all. One suspects Euripides of being a commentator and protester; certainly *The Trojan Women,* coming as it did after Athens' slaughter of the independent and neutral Melians, seems meant as a charge against the war party in Athens, and the character of Jason in *Medea* is clearly a picture of the callous and overconfident Athenian of the age. Henrik Ibsen made his fame in tragic and serious drama whose issues were issues of the time; as father of the new drama, he had many successors. The Breughels, Hogarth, Daumier pop to my mind first among many whose pictures were often social comment, and I suppose many of the religious painters had personal contemporary reference—as, surely, Dante filled his *Commedia* with it.

There has, then, been a good deal of art that is commentary and that we take as commentary, art which was made primarily to express an opinion about society or the world in general. There has likewise been a good deal of art we can call "studies." There was the "ash can" school of painting in New York with more or less realistic pictures of slums and saloons and such. Once or twice a year the best-seller list seems to be headed for weeks by a book that describes the life of senators or college professors or call girls or colored people. This has been a longtime habit of fiction, at least from Petronius, through Elizabethans like Greene and Nashe, to Defoe, Dickens, Zola, and on to Norris and Dreiser and Sinclair Lewis and us. The mark of such books is the dominance of sociological data, and Sinclair Lewis' *Babbitt* remains the best picture of Midwestern culture we have produced. Such books have been written as studies and have been read as studies. This is not to say such books may not have fictional manner and arrangement and produce some of the effects of fiction. Nor is it to say that they are necessarily objective and "scientific," for most have begun, I imagine, from the author's indignation or amusement at what he has come on. They win their plaudits, however, as "pictures of," hold attention for a dozen months, and end up finally in contemporary history courses in college.

The battles of the commentators and protesters tend to die out. The art they produce has its day. Yet some of it survives, can still be read, can still be played. Ibsen's *Ghosts,* written to show the need of doing something about syphilis, no longer arouses us about that issue, but the structure of the play is almost the structure of *Oedipus Rex* (and both are versions of the whodunit), so that its vitality as tragedy remains. Molière was angry at doctors in *The Imaginary Invalid* (oddly enough he knew he was ill and died while acting it); whatever sentiment about doctors one has now, I imagine few people, not even doctors themselves, can avoid the tension of somewhat sadistic delight as the apothecary creeps on the stage with an enormous syringe to give the protagonist an enema. Many of the points that Daumier wished to make have lost their relevance to us, yet the arrangement of light and dark and shape and direction toward his point make him still an admirable artist.

What I am suggesting is that the commentator is an artist not because of his subject matter, but because of his artistry. However just we may think the commentary at the time, however we read it first as sociology, it will not be long before we read it as a structure of another sort: "I never knew the man, but it's a darned fine picture."

That third man, who was not trying to relate the portrait to any particular person or to make it say something about that person as its primary point, was not looking only at shapes of features and head and shoulders and background. He was aware of the character of the person pictured; indeed, perhaps the major activity he went through in looking at the portrait was the process from the question "what is he?" through the piecing together of pictured characteristics until the whole became a satisfactory and complete person for him. Shape and color as well as eye or lip would suggest personality; set of head, character of shoulders, kind of clothes, background setting, all may have helped to make that unity of character.

Thus the man who saw the portrait as a darned fine picture was seeing what the others saw but was seeing it not as a reflection of something outside, but as a thing in itself, sufficient in and of itself. So from the journey outward through my own thoughts that Van Gogh's picture may produce, through the different and small-scale cosmic vision the Japanese haiku induces, I return to the shoes in one case and to the village under the snow in the other. When I look now I "know" more about both; the remnants of my feelings remain, half-conscious, and out of them has come my sense of the vital being of the things themselves. We catch ourselves saying from time to time, "That chair has personality!" We are hardly aware what we mean, but we are recognizing a being that is itself unique, "like" nothing else in the world.

"But," you will say, "suppose the artist sets out to state the truth, not some passing comment of his time, but the eternal and everlasting truth." I shall have to speak of truth several times again, but here, too. A great many artists, I imagine, have set out to tell the truth. Creation stories, tribal histories, religious myths, of course, had such intention. Few people nowadays read the journey of Odysseus as a winter journey to the underworld to bring back the new year's sun; even the late bards who sang the tale seem to have forgotten its religious meaning. The *Odyssey* becomes a story for us and seems to have been so for sixth-century Athens, though used as a mine of quotable aphorisms and examples. *Beowulf* was clearly a pagan myth of the struggle of man to escape death, but the version we have of it was put down by a Christian, and the tale becomes a story of moving but fantastic events.

If one examines King Lear, he will discover, I think, that Shakespeare wished to exhibit the "bond" of nature, that such moral law as filial piety could not be thrust out for expediency, as Edmund tried to do, without the world's destruction. He was concerned about an eternal truth. Is it this that makes the play great? Do we go through it murmuring from time to time, "How true!" or do we, most of us, accept immediately in Cordelia's case the value of blood relationship and so immediately find ourselves on Cordelia's side against Goneril and Regan, who begin at the end of the first act to be unfilial? We know what Shakespeare is saying; we have already accepted it; the play moves, I think, on our preacceptance of its theme.

A writer like Dante, however, set out to describe the Christian world and to state the truth about it. He was not Thomas Aquinas in intention, of course, and was never sainted for his work, but the *Commedia* was meant to be truth. It is remarkable in its construction, in its ordering even of its minutest parts, yet we cannot avoid the feeling that it's always saying something. What remains of it in general meaning may be the individual scenes: Paolo and Francesca, Ugolino, the trip on the back of Geryon, Dante meeting Beatrice, the great swirling rose of Mary, and so on; and a nonbeliever with little sense of the Christian tradition may read—or skip—the speeches that explain the theology as the way these characters happen to talk. The theology is there, however—and in most editions a plethora of explanatory notes—and it frequently becomes hard to see it as literature or feel it as a fascinating fantasy. We are too close to it in time, too much in its tradition to treat it as we treat the journey of Odysseus. Perhaps we will feel the shift of mind from the way we accept the scenes to the way we regard the speeches and the religious implications; that shift, I would suggest, marks the way we look at art and the way we look at nonart. If, however, you refuse to deny the *Commedia* the quality of art throughout, you will dispute self-sufficiency as a necessary attribute of art.

Certainly the artist who depends upon our feeling for the enduring characteristics of man stands more chance of immortality than the commentator who depends upon pictures of his contemporary times. The statement of great truths is not, however, very exciting; we have heard that jealousy is evil and need not go to *Othello* to find that out. The confirmation of our attitudes toward truth may be powerful, and the structuring of a derivation of a truth from characters and incidents may be fascinating; you will notice, however, that here I use adjectives of effect, "powerful" and "fascinating," and I suggest by them that the purpose of the truth is for the art, not for its own sake.

I said at the opening of this chapter that self-sufficiency, the dependency of art on itself, would be arguable. It is not a dispute I wish to be dogmatic about. I could suggest art's order makes it artificial and not like life, that it is the order we finally demand. I could suggest, niggling, that if we do not see art as self-sufficient, we do not see it artistically, but I must admit many find it truthful and value its truth and perhaps refuse to accept it unless it works with a theme they regard as important. They wish the art they are willing to call great to be "about something." I think I would insert a word: to be *greatly* about something, and hope the difference becomes clear.

At any rate, if self-sufficiency be an attribute of art—and I regard it so—it is an attribute that comes from how we take it. We do not want to use art; not as document, not as picture of, not as opinion of, not even as purveyor of truth. The documentary qualities are easy to speak of and to put into words; contrariwise, one's way of seeing art may be quite wordless. We want to see it, hear it, come to the end of it, complete it, whatever journeys of the mind it makes us take, until we comprehend it, know it, recognize its being. I think this is the way we look and act.

An artist may say during the process of his work, "That's the way it goes," meaning that's the way a leg curves or a line runs or the way you put into words a heron's flight; but when at the end he leans back and says, "That's right," I suggest he is not feeling experience or order or self-sufficiency or truth, but only feeling art. And we, too.

CHAPTER 5

The Internal Meanings of Art

THE ARTIST, I have suggested, uses his experience to make an orderly thing whose very orderliness gives art its own self-sufficiency. He has himself, in making it, looked at it, read it, listened to it, felt it. He has been his own audience; he knows by now, perhaps, what he wanted to do, and though almost always unsatisfied—so that he often says, "That's the best I can do!"—he is finished. He may or may not want another audience; most artists do, not only because they must sell to live but because they are social and egotistic as most of us are. The artist's relation with his public, however, tends to stop with the presentation of the piece of art, for what the audience sees is the art and not the artist. We as audience may, of course, run down enigmatic things, as I did with Blake's "Chapel of Gold," and have to hunt back through the artist's life and work to find out things like what chapel and what snake, but that is not usual. The audience is other psyches, and what they find may or may not have been what the artist intended them to find. Shakespeare, I am sure, would be thoroughly flabbergasted to read all that has been written in the last nearly four centuries about what he "meant."

What the audience in any way finds I want to call "meaning." Each member of the artist's audience goes through an experience of some sort; that experience is the meaning of the work to that member. Each reader, listener, playgoer, viewer will have an experience different in some degree, for each will have a different past and hence a different character. Thus each piece of art may have a myriad possible meanings; yet men are more alike than different; most Americans like steak and ice cream, and I feel pretty sure that those members of humankind who have never had either could, with a little practice, become fond of both. (Which may, of course, be only my provincial prejudice.) Thus I think we can speak in a general way about meanings and even speak in a general way about the meanings of a given piece of work.

The first thing a piece of art means is what immediately happens to us, what pops into our brains, the product of subject matter. "The cat climbed up the tree" must bring certain visual sights to you, another cat than mine, another tree than mine, and a different speed and distance up the tree, but something. So, "I saw a chapel all of gold" will bring sight to us out of our memories, for we have seen chapels and gold. If Blake had written, "I saw a charabanc of cinnabar," we would have some trouble, for we would not know, perhaps, that a charabanc is a bus and cinnabar a kind of rock, and even if we did, we could not put the two together, and satisfactory meaning would not come to us. When the pictures succeed in our minds, they are the primary stuff of meaning, and they can be fascinating in themselves. I sit often in summer on a hill over a pond that goes into the ocean, and watch boats go by. Just watching them is fun; the mind is kept busy. True, description of them in words would not be so effective. The nineteenth-century novelists often felt that it was good to describe natural settings; nowadays we find any exact description of sights in words likely to be only distracting, yet we can enjoy a certain length of travel picture, and some of us can endure even quite a number of a friend's colorslides of his Western trip.

So even an "abstract" picture like this of Kandinsky's will stimulate us with its variety of colors and shapes (Figure 7). Perhaps here variety and contrast are important, yet slighter variations, even a cloudy merging of factors, can be effective, too. One may say that Kandin-

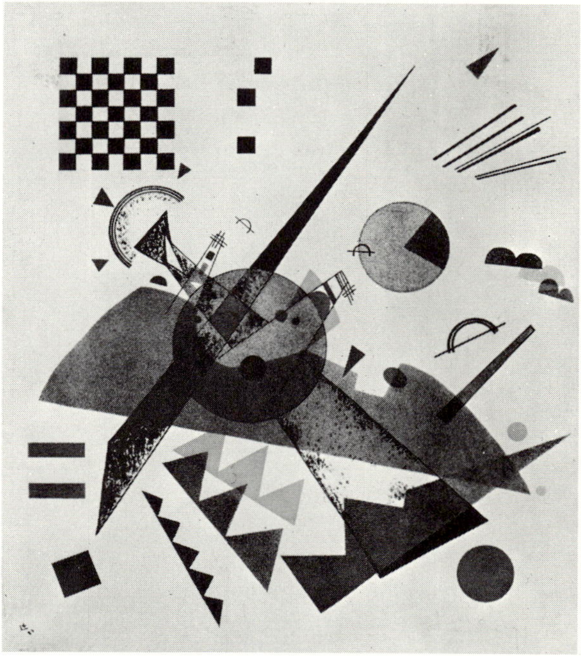

FIGURE 7. "Composition with Chessboard," lithograph and stencil by Wassily Kandinsky. Courtesy of the Museum of Fine Arts, Boston

sky's kind of stimulation of the eye is analogous to music's stimulation of the ear; there is no external imitation at all: Bach does not sound like moving water or female conversation, though we speak of the "voices" in his fugues. There is, of course, in both poetry and prose something analogous to abstract colors and the usual abstraction of music: there is sound. Some of it is created by repetition of like sounds:

When to the sessions of sweet silent thought . . .[1]

Some of it is created by a repetition of words:

. . . Love is not love
Which alters when it alteration finds,
Or bends with the remover to remove.[1]

Some of it is created by repetition of grammatical structures:

To err is human, to forgive divine.[2]

In prose it is often created by the placing and balancing of phrases and clauses, so that our inexplicable sense of length and weight is satisfied:

The cotton was long since picked and ginned, and all day now the wagons loaded with gathered corn moved between field and crib, processional across the enduring land.[3]

All these examples are strengthened as in music by a metrical base, a regularity of emphasis greater in verse than in prose but still active in the rhythms of prose. And we react to meter by a psychological participation called empathy.

Though we may visually see the repetition of "s" in the first example, and the repetition of form in "to err" and "to forgive" in the third, and though we may feel the intellectual contrast of these two phrases, most musical effects in nonmusical arts work on us only half consciously, I think, for the center of our attention may be on something else. This does not mean that one cannot almost chant "When to the sessions of sweet silent thought/I summon up remembrance of things past" (out of fifty or sixty separate sounds here, depending on how you want to count, there are nine "s" sounds, five "t" sounds, five or six "n" sounds, three "m" sounds, four "uh" unaccented sounds, and so on, which means a very considerable patterning), and in chanting, one speaks for the music as against the meaning so that one hardly knows what he is saying. These effects may be increased by ease of saying, so that the stimulus to, if not the actual operation of, the muscles of speech moves with ease from sound to sound, phrase to phrase. Sound works on us almost without our knowing it, but works nevertheless.

These meanings, sights and sounds, I take to be immediate. We need not struggle for them, provided only we have enough knowledge to recognize words or shapes. I have attempted to describe them as coming, so far, without much subjectively attached to them. It will often be true, however, that a subjective response will come simultaneously. The second effect of them then—or the third, if you wish to count sound—is what is awakened out of our past feeling about them. Thus both "chapel" and "gold" will draw reactions, attitudes we have previously had. I suggested both seemed good and both seemed valuable; others may disagree, for they may have prejudices "against" rather than "for" these, yet most of us will take them as symbols for something good.

Meanings of this sort are not individual and unrelated, of course; they enter the successive web of logic, for we are not gullets down which experience is simply poured, but psyches with remembrances and with ways of thought. Suppose we try a small sentence: "Yesterday the first daffodil came out." It might have been found in an old diary. There is sight, the daffodil blooming. We may be very fond of daffodils or not, but what comes then will not be a reaction to daffodils so much as a reaction to "the first" (try "a" instead). I think I feel coming up in me the hope that spring brings: the winter and its often unpleasant connotations are over. I am not yet to that looking back of Onitsura's poem or of Herrick's moralizing. This is the first of spring, and all that spring means to me may come out, triggered by the contrast in "first."

Not all things bring such meaning. It would be hard to find much of it coming out of "Yesterday I scratched my ear." It is remarkable, for instance, how few paintings of automobiles there are, and though I like steak, the photographs of steaks some advertisers try to tease us with have very little meaning for me. We are not all of us equally attached to anything, I suppose, but some things are likely to bring more past feeling than others, and the art of being dull is the art of bringing up things few people feel much about, pro or con.

Much of the effect of a poem like Eliot's "The Hollow Men" comes from his reiterated use of words that suggest lifelessness, sterility: straw, scarecrow, rat's feet, broken glass, broken columns, fading star, jawbone. These are not strong feelings that come, but they have just the tone to make us feel the "hollowness" of whomever it is Eliot is criticizing in this poem.

In fiction, in the story, novel, narrative poem, or play, one of the chief subjective meanings is our response to the characters. In the early tale, folk tale, fairy story, fabliau, in such a tale as the Kutenai animal one, the character of the actor is unimportant. It is hard to avoid some sort of sentiment about a human actor of a fable, but we need not be very much attached to him or very much hate him. This is true, too, of ritual drama and perhaps of heroic tales and those compilations from old myth we call epics. Later, more extensive and more realist fiction, however, has increased its meanings for us by our sentiments for or against characters. It is popular nowadays to say we "identify." This does not, I take it, imply that we put ourselves in the character's place in any real way, but that we feel, in ourselves but not for ourselves, hopes, fears, tensions toward the things in the book the character feels toward. This, I suppose, is sympathy. It is seldom that such feelings become feelings for ourselves. James Joyce maintained, as I remember it, that at the crisis of tragedy our pity outward for the tragic figure suddenly shifts to our terror for ourselves in face of the forces of the world he faces. This may be so; at that moment we must drop the tragic figure out of mind, cease to identify or sympathize. Our agony supersedes our sight of his. I imagine the experience is rare. I never take the place of Oedipus or Antigone or Othello or Lear. Such replacement as Joyce suggests might be unendurable. The tragedy seems to me to work on a less personal plane; the protagonist may be admirable but not lovable, as we should not be made, by too sweet an actress, to love Cordelia; knowing more and foreseeing more than the protagonist, we cannot quite make his tensions ours; it is in this "ironic" situation that tragedy goes on, and it should not be confused by overplaying the protagonist's nobility, virtue, kindness so that we "identify" with him.

It was the comedy or the successful play and story that made the chief character one whose tensions we could feel. It is through such heightening of our tensions that novels have increased their meanings to us. The recent "antinovels" with "antiheroes" have recognized that the former novel's excess of sympathy and antipathy could only lead to illogical and melodramatic conclusions. The substitution of protagonists who draw feelings neither pro nor con, such as Meursault in Camus's *The Stranger* or Rabbit in Updike's *Rabbit, Run,* has produced a meaning of flabbiness and insignificance except as these novels may be taken as commentaries on the world and society.

It is these meanings deriving from our attachments to the characters that grow and change through the passage of a piece of fiction. They enrich the total order of the piece and can hardly be separated from it. They may form an order, a beginning and an end in themselves, but that order may not be the most notable of the elements of a story's design. In a sense they are as immediate as the sights and sounds and remembrances of feeling.

The means of such meanings may be extremely subtle. I remember walking with a friend around an exhibition room and stopping before a portrait. It was a picture of a blond young man, one whom one would superficially like, but we both found him unpleasant, arrogant, and wondered why. We decided that the effect was created by a very small change of curve in the left half of his upper lip, a matter of, perhaps, one thirty-second of an inch; one thirty-second of an inch less lip, and he would have been pleasant, at least noncommittal; now he was arrogant. We are all aware that a photographer can "murder you" by the wrong light, the wrong angle, the wrong momentary tension of muscles. And in the Chekhov story of the theological student I mentioned before, Chekhov checks our acceptance of the enthusiasm of the youth's happiness at belonging in time by a phrase, "he was only twenty-two," perhaps even by the one word "only." We can suddenly hear the older man judging the younger and making us follow. A great deal of the technical craft of an artist derives from the awareness of such meanings.

This sort of meaning, from our reactions to colors and shape to our sentiments about "God, country, and Yale," is a major meaning of the experience of art. Perhaps we can call it the meaning of texture; we speak of it as rich or delicate or stark or bland and so on, words which express, I suppose, something of the amount and something of the quality of the feelings evoked from us. Poets especially have tried to extend this evocative power of what they speak of; first by adjectives and adverbs, then by various figures of speech. So the poet goes from "the sky was blue" to the "sky was glaring blue," originally an animist figure, to "the sky was blue as the mantle of the Madonna," and, sometimes incomprehensibly, to "the mantle of the Madonna glared." Two things are put together: we see A and then are turned to B and back again, bringing our feeling about B—glaring, mantle, Madonna—back with us. Such couplings come from primitive peoples—calling a piece of string "cotton woman"—and they come from civilized ones. They increase the quantity of experience, the plain number of neurons that is aroused, and they often have such a faculty of relating the hitherto unrelated that we feel a sudden illumination. Though they are not, I think, the chief meaning in art, they are so attractive that many a poem has been "made" by them.

When in disgrace with fortune and men's eyes
I all alone beweep my outcast state,
And trouble deaf heaven with my bootless cries,
And look upon myself, and curse my fate . . .[4]

We cannot stop there, for we are dominated by the simple rhetorical word "when," but our minds have certainly been enriched.

These meanings that pop into the head with their connotations I would like to include in immediate meanings. They are meanings, in part, of subject matter; a picture of a lake is a picture of a lake; one goes through this picture to the scene. Yet no picture of a thing can avoid waking recollections, old feelings, nostalgias. Thus no meaning can be thoroughly divorced from our subjective responses, can be as clear as the word "immediate" may suggest. Such meanings of the passing texture of art, of the subject matter of art, are those many people are chiefly aware of. "Trouble deaf heaven" may make us aware how nice it is as a phrase; the lake may seem cool and its prospect delightful. We become warmed by such meanings, and for many readers and viewers such meanings may seem the most art can give.

Still, the "when" of rhetoric holds in our psyches: we need a motion further; we come back from our imagined plunge in the lake and look about us and feel other pulls of shape and color. The meanings of these desires and tensions, the meanings of design and order, may pull us half-aware. If I say they are dominant, I do not mean that any "when" clause answered by its "then" will make a poem good. A richly wrought "when" will pull more from us than a colorless one, of course; order may be easier to manage than texture; yet order may shape us at last more than texture can. Order may be a more important meaning.

I have said the psychic curve of design may be "fun"; it may be a very grim, a very heartrending fun. The artist may design intellectually for problem, development, solution; he may also design, I think, for emotional reactions: question, curiosity, tension, fear, hope, suspense, absorption, satisfaction. The possible orderings of our response are myriad, but all, if art be art, I should say, will be molded on some version of the psychic curve, whose exercise is fun. The larger the piece, the more chance for variety and duplication of responses; yet the shape must finally come clear and the curve be completed.

There are stories that depend upon action, on a decisive battle, struggle, decision, and its outcome. The meaning of such a story reduces itself at last to the meaning of our anticipation and foresight of decision and our feeling afterward. To a degree, all fairy stories are of this sort, and all stories of the great West. Though any experienced reader knows that virtue must triumph, that our hero and heroine will be happy ever after, yet even this foreknowledge does not conquer forefeeling, and suspense and resultant relief and satisfaction may be gripping. It is for this version of the psychic curve that many readers read and many patronize the cinema. The length of a love story is almost entirely dependent on the number and complexity of the obstructions that extend the middle between boy sees girl and boy gets girl; yet what we want is their junction.

This is the bourgeois or middle-class story, of course, but it goes back a long way in history. In the hands of the author whose fame has endured, two variants have been played: in one the boy doesn't get the girl or is unsatisfied with the girl he gets, the customary design of a writer like Henry James, whose psychic drive seems always to have found the climax unsatisfactory; in the other the middle assumes such variety and impressiveness that the final accommodation of boy and girl seems unimportant, as in Cervantes or Fielding, and even, I am afraid, in the romantic comedies of Shakespeare. Too many small versions of the psychic curve can rob the major design of its power but may themselves arouse satisfactions of a quantity and of a quality that justify fame. It is the habit of the novel, I think, to act this way: at the end of D. H. Lawrence's *Lady Chatterley's Lover,* hero and heroine are about to be married, but our psyches are exhausted from their previous sexual junctions, and the final legal sanction seems unimportant—though in some way necessary to complete the design and to complete our response.

In earlier times, though seldom now, the design depended not on the suspense of alternatives—would he, or wouldn't he?—but on what I can only call the suspense of the inevitable. The design led forward by its feeling and its events toward a climactic act; yet the climactic act held no question, only certainty. This was the design of the ritual drama as you can see it done by the fifth-century Greeks: Agamemnon, Oedipus, Antigone do not have alternatives in our minds; their doom is plain from the beginning; indeed, is planned for by the building up of our sentiments through speech and choral song. Yet the foregone holds us with the fascination of watching the inevitable happen. For some readers the detective story and the Western take on this ritual character, being themselves so conventional as to be ritualistic in order. It is not the event that matters but the process of catching the criminal, the building of fact upon fact that will lead to that catching. Here again, though, the end must be there; we would not be happy until the end was reached to satisfy us. Attractive and absorbing as the development may be, we must have the final cadence to feel complete.

This so far has gone to suggest the sights and feelings of immediate meanings and the emotional attachments of order in time. Order, however, may succeed without such emotionally remembered and related attachments at all. Let me illustrate the effect of "pure" order by returning to Pueblo pots. Here is one whose bowl is roughly round and whose neck is large and tall (Figure 8). We feel the swell of the bowl out and in and the rise of the neck; there is little surprise here; our eyes go very rapidly around and up. I think I feel that the neck is so tall and heavy that the whole thing is a little unsteady. I wonder what use that extent of neck is. I am not very effectively worked on or satisfied. The one I used before (Figure 1) is different. There the upward, outward curve of the bowl, after going up and over its outmost point, comes inward more sharply, more summarily. If its curves were reversed, we would get a mushroom shape, a closing down, depressing, perhaps; as it is, it has some feel of rise and finish, not so much as we would get in Persian or Chinese work, but something of vigor. The top curve comes in to the neck, and the neck rises straight, with a little outburst at the top, a lip to end it. There is relation of neck to body more reasonable and more stable than in the first bowl. If shorter, the neck would not suggest the closed quality of the bowl; if narrower, it would seem too small for the body of the bowl, as the head and neck of a guinea hen look absurd on its body (other races,

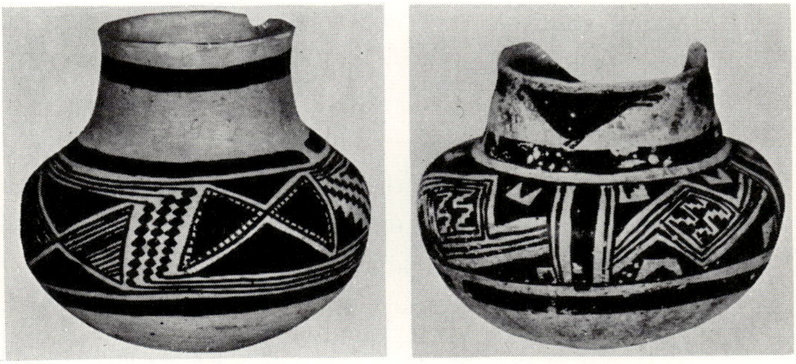

FIGURE 8. Two Jars from Homolovi, Arizona. Courtesy of the Chicago Natural History Museum

to be sure, have made use of that relationship). Do you want the decoration only on the upper curve of the bowl or to go over and down? Pueblo potters used both methods; perhaps decoration on only half of the bowl gives more vitality to its sense of rise. Here the decoration, made of very oblique triangles, carries one's eye around the bowl. Do the long triangles lift you spirally toward the neck? They may also, as your attention goes to the right, carry you down. Either motion is jagged and stimulating. When one's eye rises, the small checker design at the top of the neck tends to be a stopping point, scattering motion.

On the right-hand bowl of Figure 8 the decoration is broken by uprights which halt the motion of our eyes and may carry it inward to the neck. The body of the jar lifts up more firmly than the last; the inward slanting neck, larger at the bottom than the last, pulls the eyes in as it rises, tends to finish off the design. The turkeys made by a few squiggles on the triangular shape tend to halt one's eye. This bowl works with less circular and more up-and-down effects than the last.

If your mind has been jogged by what it sees and has been moved outward, inward, up, and its feelings of size and direction related, if it has been held and moved by the painted designs, you will have been through an experience and reached a feeling for the wholeness, the unity, the being of these bowls. Motion and tension have been at work and a resolution reached in the process of looking—not happily reached for me in the first bowl, differently satisfied in the latter two.

Even when a great amount of memory and fancy is evoked, design may be the factor that calls out and brings together. Let me quote the most famous of Japanese haiku, Basho's little poem:

Old pond:
Frog-jump-in
Water-sound.[5]

This is an incident, I think it is clear, of a summer evening, made of two nouns, the second with another noun and active suggestions in its hyphenated adjective. The journey I take from this has gone a number of ways over the years I have recited this little bit, but I think I always see a dark pond just over some rushes; I hear the sound; then I see the ripples spreading on the pond. I understand some Zen Buddhists stop here, regarding the frog's leap as a devotee's into satori, or enlightenment. For me the contrasts begin: silence-sound, stillness-motion, darkness-greenness, age-youth, immortal-mortal, inanimate-animate, until my mind pops up with the very ancient inanimate world, volcanic like the pictures in a geology text, and into this world leaps—young, smiling, bright green now—the vitality and the aggressive and inconsequential impertinence of the young frog. I am reminded of Faulkner's Nobel Prize speech, wherein, after the last dingdong of doom, there remains the sound of mankind chattering. Then all this fades, and I come back to the silent old pond, the fact, unified.

This is more me than Basho, perhaps, yet a few words may evoke a world of meaning. How much of this Basho "meant" no one seems to know. Perhaps I am being untrue to him: certainly three hundred years ago he had not heard of Faulkner and probably had not seen a geology text; his words set my mind going, though, and I hold him responsible. He does this with a minimum of design, really only the contrast of pond and sound. It is so small a poem you could say it could hardly avoid design, but it does have the contrast that sets my mind going.

Surely we cannot keep taking such mental journeys through a play or a novel or even a short story; there is not time while hearing a play or while reading a story, unless we read very slowly indeed. With reseeing and rereading, a playwright like Shakespeare will show how thick his language is, how suggestive scenes and confrontations of character are. There is never so much "world" as in Basho's few syllables, however, and indeed should not be. Extent of evocation from very little is compensated by less extent from many more proddings of our minds. Over and over again Molière makes us dislike Tartuffe, each time from relation to a different character or from a different sight of his effect on the stupid good man, Orgon. So Aeschylus in *Agamemnon,* if we read him right, builds bit by bit a fear of doom that becomes close to explicit in the powerful vision of Cassandra. In both plays, of course, movement and tone of voice, "acting," evoke quite as much meaning from us as the words do. Each, however, batters over and over on our brains.

It is inevitable that such effects narrow the area worked. A story, though it wish to make us feel the solidity of the whole world, cannot speak of everything in the world, spreading its shots. It must assume sooner or later some of the concentration of Basho's little verse. When the process of design is as simple as a boy and girl story, or when it has great complexity and its effects are too subtle for its creator to be aware of, the curve of our own attention must narrow to an end; all must converge and center.

If you look at all the breadth of people and ideas that Dostoevsky presents in *The Brothers Karamazov* and your various feelings about them, your curiosities, fears, likes, and dislikes, you will see that these come to bear on Dmitri's trial. We have felt for—and perhaps against

—each of the brothers, have gone through the suspense of "will there be murder?" and the long curious history of "who did it?" The trial becomes in a way an emotional anticlimax but takes on a more mechanical and intellectual suspense: we must have the answer to what happens to Dmitri. I find, myself, that the simple curiosity about that, through those long speeches by the attorneys, mounts very high. My responses have been spread and then centralized on the murder, been spread again and once more centralized on the question of the murderer, then shifted in their tone to the days in the courtroom, the coming together of Dmitri and Grushenka, the verdict I know unjust and yet deserved. It is a book of rich and stimulating texture, whose parts are almost whole novels in themselves; at the least it takes thirty hours to read; it narrows and concentrates at last.

One of the agencies of such narrowing is likely to be the tone, the character of the author, his particular way of looking at the world. Whatever each of us has as character is shifted a little, concentrated, made consistent by the manner of the author. The strong brushstrokes of Cézanne or Van Gogh, the lighting of Rembrandt, even the gold undertone of Titian at his best, do the same thing. They channel our responses.

The phenomenon of emotion, which no one seems yet to understand at all, seems to me to be structured as such wide or repeated evocation and then its narrowing, concentrating, centralizing, as if all the energy of the various awakened cells of the brain shot their energy into one spot, one area of intensity. Granted, this is not all remembered emotion, such as comes at the mention of things that have been dear to us; it is created emotion, new emotion, built out of our pasts but also built out of the past of this piece of art: all our feelings about Dmitri are there concentrated at the end. The past pieces are not black or white; they are various, not so much contradictory as balanced out, so that no one is hero, no one is villain, no act fully horrid, but all are, I think, powerfully built. It is the past of our experience before the book, our past *in* the book, that floods to its center. All the hints, all our feelings about the characters in *Agamemnon* are simple, uniform in a way, directed toward action however cryptically, and then, as I have found out from experience, the three cries of Agamemnon as he is murdered offstage (very hard for an actor to get right) are almost sexually emotional, like the climax of a bullfight. The effect is less narrow, less stark in Dostoevsky's book, less narrow, perhaps, in Shakespeare's work, but not less finally impressive.

One of the most powerful meanings that art can bring comes out of this sort of bringing together. It is manifest in a small way, I suppose, in such a poem as this of Emily Dickinson's:

The soul selects her own society,
Then shuts the door;
On her divine majority
Obtrude no more.

Unmoved, she notes the chariot's pausing
At her low gate;
Unmoved, an emperor is kneeling
Upon her mat.

I've known her from an ample nation
Choose one;
Then close the valves of her attention
Like stone.[6]

From the general of the first stanza we go to the example of the second and the particular of the third. Here from the spread of the word "ample" (the best word in the language for that spot, by the way) we narrow down to one. Then we "close"—"like stone." The abrupt two syllables, the long "o," the whole association of stone with graveyards give a tomblike sound, and suddenly, I think, I shift into a sense of utter finality, of the choice endless and changeless, of human decision irrevocable and eternal. Verse form does it, sound does it, the words do it; their concentration on "stone" suddenly shifts me into a version of "illumination." It is a short poem; there are not many beatings at my psyche; it is Emily Dickinson's skill that she manages so much with so little. Its shift of me is not greatly moving, perhaps, as I am not so likely to be greatly moved in front of painting, but it moves and it illumines.

The same sort of meaning, the sudden pulling together into illumination, may occur at any point in a piece of literature. It is the effect of the happy phrase, especially the product of poetry. I met it recently in leafing through an anthology hunting for something else; all of a sudden a piece of a stanza popped out of Byron's "Isles of Greece":

> *I see their glorious black eyes shine*
> . . . .
> *To think such breasts must suckle slaves.*[7]

I felt the summary concentration and sight of poetry. It was not much, or great, or about a cosmos, but about Greece under the Turks. I find the same property now and again in prose; for instance, the sentence in Malory's *Mort d'Arthur:* "And so departed Lancelot from the court forever." All the hopes and accomplishments and failures of Arthur and Lancelot are brought to a sad center on that sentence.

Perhaps the greatest single scene in American literature comes at the end of Faulkner's "The Bear." This is a story of the destruction of nature, the woods and its animals, and the destruction of humankind; it is also the story of the growing up of a boy. There is the boy, Ike McCaslin, and the bear, Old Ben, and the bear's hunting year after year. Faulkner makes the bear seem immortal, enduring, the spirit of wild nature. Ike's growing up draws on the rituals of tribesmen, the clan uncle Sam Fathers, the meeting with the bear as totem grandfather in a strangely tingling scene, Ike's growth in the tribal skills of the woods till the woods and nature are his mother. Then Ike feels the upcoming last hunting of the bear as the final act of a drama. Old Ben is killed, sharp before our sight, killed as nature is being despoiled by lumbering and farming man, but also as a ritual bear is killed, over and over in recurrent immortality; and with his killing, Sam Fathers is stricken and soon dies, to be given a funeral Indian fashion. Two springs later Ike comes back to the foursquare burial mound where the bear's paw is buried over the bones of the dog who held him and where Sam Fathers is buried now. As Ike passes across the grave, he thinks of Sam Fathers, aware of his presence, of Sam and Old Ben, now part of the earth but deathless as they become a new and myriad life in the earth's ecology. He meets a snake, head held high as his knee, old symbol of evil. "Chief: grandfather," he says, echoing the Indian totem greeting; the snake walks away in an almost human fashion from the fulfilled young man. Nature, its spirits and its past, man and his profound membership in nature, death and the continuance of life, the world's evil—all meet here in the mind of Ike McCaslin and the mind of the reader. Suddenly, all this shifts into a cosmos of overwhelming emotion.

I suppose I am sympathetic to this sort of view, but I can read philosophic statements of the construct and not be moved or given "revelation" at all. Faulkner's story works with me every time, the fifteen or twenty times I have read it. This means, I take it, that the process counts, as it does in music or in games or in sex. It also illustrates the emotional shift into illumination, the coming together into one conviction of all that has preceded and all that has been evoked of our memories, feelings, attitudes. A unity is made. When one really "sees" Basho's little frog leap, the implications of the small incident, perhaps the same thing occurs; perhaps this *is* satori. At any rate, the final unity is the most powerful meaning in art, I think. It is the final meaning toward which design has worked. "For thy sweet love remember'd such wealth brings/That then I scorn to change my state with kings"—this is the conclusion of Shakespeare's sonnet, its summation; perhaps it does not move even as much as Emily Dickinson's poem, but it does have some shift into unity, satisfaction, the feeling of having "got there."

The illumination or revelation is often indescribable, for it may not come to words at all. A few years ago I saw the Grand Canyon for the first time. I had seen postcards, slides, movies, paintings of it. Suddenly there it was, looking just *like* a postcard. It took me some considerable time and a good many different views of it to see it for itself and as itself. I could bring to it some sense of geology, some memory of other gorges, some early learned fear of heights, some speculation of the first man, the first Indian, who came up through the forest of fir to its brim, some sense of the earth's age and man's recency. These passed through my brain and went away, and piece by piece I saw eroded earth and peninsulas of earth and layers of earth and a small trail below and the small rivers and the colors and the spread of distance, and these, too, went away as parts, and suddenly there was the Grand Canyon. What did it mean? It meant G–E–E!—heartfelt but devoid now of anything you could call an idea.

So, when I reach, at the end of the *Iliad*, "Such was the funeral of Hector, tamer of horses," as I have done once a year for many years now, I find myself wordless, overwhelmed but wordless. Such meaning, if it comes, is some sort of summary of all the other meanings, of the whole experience of a piece of art.

That whole meaning will be made of many little meanings. At times in large works, novels, epics, symphonies, we may find what seem contradictions; we may run on blind ends. So the long excursions following Alyosha and Ivan, Dmitri's brothers, the relations of Alyosha and the young girl, may seem as causes of action unnecessary in Dostoevsky's long novel. It is hard to say how they fit or why they are needed, yet most readers will not want to take them out. Only the scenes with the teen-age Kolya seem not to count. Our responses, of course, will be baffled and diminished by the illogical and inconsequent. However inconsequent "life" may be, no considerable work of art is likely to mimic this property of life, for logic is the guide of our response. And logic and consequence derive their being in part from what has gone before but also in the foresights and forefeelings they set up. They are consequent in their coming from somewhere and in their going somewhere; they are finally justified in their having got somewhere. Achilles and Agamemnon, divided by Achilles' wrath, are brought together by an act, the killing of Patroclus, which will have another consequence, the slaughter of Hector, and this, in turn, will lead to the final book, the sorrow of Priam and Hecuba and Andromache and Helen, and so end what the opening lines of the epic portended, the deaths of many men and the sorrows of their deaths.

Logic is not only the logic of act but of feeling, and to satisfy us wholly the two must jibe. So the story in which by rights the foolhardy hero should be murdered—the run-of-the-mill detective story is built this way—does not answer that "by rights" but saves him for the sake of our feelings, and this failure of the two logics to jibe lessens the meaning of the story.

There are meanings evoked from our past experience, as the artist called them out of his, all the attitudes, feelings, sympathies, and revulsions we come to art with and that fasten around the new things presented to us. There are the developments of these by the order of the piece of art, the building into new experience, the exercises of our psyches in the curve of our attention from beginning through middle to end, from question through ways of answer to satisfaction. And there are the concluding meanings, from G–E–E at the Grand Canyon to a milder *m-m-m*, perhaps, at a Pueblo bowl, which express the being, the selfhood of the whole.

These meanings, the immediate and textural, and those of order and design are the major internal meanings of art.

"A poem should not mean but be," Archibald MacLeish wrote, and we can perhaps ask, "How can a bowl *mean* anything?" The answer, I suppose, is "How can it help mean something if you look at it?" And the bowl, if it could speak, might answer, "You mean *you* mean nothing."

CHAPTER 6

The External Meanings of Art

I HAVE attempted to show the internal meaning of art, the meanings of the experience. I fancy many will not accept these as "meanings," for when they ask "But what does it *mean?*" they are not thinking of experience but of the relation of art to the world outside it. Thus, I must say what I can about "external" meanings.

Every piece of art is a symbol, for it is not the thing itself. The relation of the art to the thing symbolized is, however, not always simple, for one may keep one's eyes and feelings on the art or one may go out to the thing symbolized, and one may do both in rapid succession. I am afraid I misused the line from Archibald MacLeish, for he was not saying that poetry has no meaning but that the internal meaning, the being, of the poem is valid and the external improper. However, we can and do consider art as presenting something valid about what it speaks of and as having a series of meanings therefore.

One must first of all distinguish such meanings from subject matter. A picture may be of a reclining nude or of seven squares, a poem of a dead lady or of the poet's feelings on waking up. These are subject matter and are internal meanings. So long as the artist seems to be speaking of particular things, perhaps we may be inclined to avoid making his art symbolic or typical. Suppose, however, the poet seems to be speaking generally —"How good to wake up in America!"—or the reclining nude seems to us to express the "essence" of female attractiveness. Do we feel the general and external dominant over the internal and particular?

The last time I was in the Museo San Marco in Florence, which is almost entirely devoted to the painting of Fra Angelico, I was singled out as a likely American tip-giver by the official guide. He showed me his own favorite face of the many Fra Angelico painted of the Virgin and in the manner of a stage performer intoned, "*Giovanissima, sanctissima, maiestissima, soavissima, celestissima*" and some other superlatives I have forgotten. I saw what he meant: these characteristics were there plain in the Virgin's face. I have little doubt that Fra Angelico meant to put those characteristics there; he was devout and full of admiration for Mary. Do these characteristics, if you find them, transfer from the picture to become a characterization of the theological Mary, or are they kept in your mind as referent only to this picture? I have raised this question before in trying to deal with the word self-sufficiency. I cannot answer for others here, I think, and my own reaction is unimportant. Some viewers will want to turn from the picture to a concept of Mary, and for them the picture means that other reference.

Suppose we take a very famous small poem by Oliver Goldsmith:

When lovely woman stoops to folly
And finds too late that men betray,

What charm can soothe her melancholy?
What art can wash her guilt away?

The only art her guilt to cover,
To hide her shame from every eye,
To give repentance to her lover,
And wring his bosom, is—to die.[1]

I suspect one's first reaction to this is to laugh. The poem is so neatly arranged; the "snapper," though foreseeable from the word "eye" that must be rhymed with, is held to the last; the whole tone refuses sentiment, evokes far less sympathy than, say, the folk song "Careless Love"; it is callous, but the final "to die" is so sudden and summary that it brings the laugh. Are you inclined to call this "true"? Is this the one answer, the "only art"? Do you begin to say, "Well, yes, but—" and think of suggesting the Florence Crittenden League or waiting for the right understanding man or getting father to wave his shotgun, which might indeed wring the bosom of the lover forced to be husband. Would these either hide guilt or make her lover repentant? Is the poem right? Or only a joke? Some way back I seem to have been hard on Whitman because his opinion about the astronomer's destruction of wonder at the stars did not seem to me to jibe with my previous experience. Do you wish to criticize Goldsmith in the same way? Must the artist be faithful to common experience of the external world and be brought to the bar of that test? Do you wish to retire from this question and admire, if you do, the skill of Goldsmith and the convincing quality of his brief poem? Do you want to repudiate the chance of external meaning?

These are questions that I have not answered, for upon their answers will depend a later stand toward life and art, and the stand toward life and art will in turn control the answers to these questions. The issue, not the solution, must be enough so far.

Some pieces of verse are pretty clearly statements, not necessarily of the poet's experience but, like Goldsmith's (he was never a lady stooped to folly), about the world. So Emily Dickinson's poem of the soul's selection of one seems a statement about human habit, and the shift into emotion I feel at it is indeed a shift into revelation, here of the possible eternity of such choice. So Robert Herrick's moralizing about fading daffodils seems more a statement that we are going to die than anything else. In elementary school I had to learn:

Life is real! Life is earnest!
And the grave is not its goal;
Dust thou art, to dust returneth
Was not spoken of the soul.

I still chant that stanza, for it has a nice singsong, and the stanza that goes:

Lives of great men all remind us
We can make our lives sublime,
And, departing, leave behind us
Footprints on the sands of time; [2]

And sometimes I use one stanza or the other as commentary on passing events. I am sure Longfellow wrote the poem as one that has an external meaning, that says something about human life, that is true *of* things. In contrast, what does the usual Western mean in this sense of "mean"? It means the bad guys went to jail and the good guys got the ranch and the girl. There is no external meaning (virtue triumphs?).

The chief external meaning, then, is a statement about

something, and the answer that is wanted by those who ask "What does it mean?" is the answer "What it says." This answer becomes interpretation, and interpretation is what a majority of the young give you when asked about a piece of art.

If we had no pasts, if we were not each of us in some way a philosopher with a view of things, we would not, perhaps, put everything we see and read up against "the world as we know it." Contrariwise, the artist would have very little except the most mechanical responses from us to work with. Art will relate to life, then; the question is, "Is that relation its most important meaning, and is knowledge, the result of such relationship, its most important function?" Again, I think the answer to these questions is one of choice, that it must come from an individual view of art. But let me try to narrow the issue.

It is certainly true that most of us want art to be *about* something. Even those most devoted to art as separate from life find it difficult to be stirred by things they have no feeling about. We do not know very much about the effects of music; it seems on the face of it nonimitative; words can hardly avoid reference; "the cat" is a cat, but what does a musical phrase bring up? During the last war the opening phrase of Beethoven's "Fifth" came to stand for an Allied victory sign, but before that—and now for those who have forgotten—did those four notes refer to anything? I think the answer, oddly, is "Yes," and I think those notes were picked for that victory sign because they did refer to something: they are an assertion, decisive and resolute. If I "translate" them into words—forgive the absurdity, but I have only words to work with—to those notes go the words "we will prevail"—among others, of course. I wish that I could relate rises and falls of intervals, harmonies, rhythms, tempi to our responses in any more than a very general way, but it is clear music works on the same psyche that other arts do, and that our feelings about things, more feelings and attitudes than things—more adjectives than nouns, if I can say it so—are some part of musical meaning. Art is veritably mixed up with our past experience, and thus we can say about music or about an abstract picture that it is slight and not "about much," or that it is "strong" or "profound." We respond to each sample of it as we respond to unimportant or impressive or very important acts, people, ideas. Does it "mean" those acts, those people, those ideas? Does it mean some statement about them? Is it, in other words, philosophy?

Art certainly persuades us to look at things in its own consistent way. The tone of a piece, the character of the artist come through, so that when I suggested that the relation of artist and public was only through the art, I did not mean to imply that the public do not feel a character they call artist behind the work. We say we like Faulkner or Picasso or Prokofiev, or such performers as Heifetz or Alec Guinness; we say we can "recognize" them every time. What we mean is a consistency of view that rides through their work. I remember that in the days when art critics were adulant of Cézanne, one critic put much of the excess about him into perspective by saying that one day all of a sudden he saw Cézanne wasn't painting this kind of greatness or that but was really only painting Cézannes. This consistency of tone, of course, is one of the agents of narrowing our response and making internal emotional meaning possible. It is also a way of making us look at the world and is, as such, a philosophic commentary. "I like the way he sees things" means, I think, that we approve of his philosophy and that his philosophy is an important part of his art.

Tone and character become, then, an inescapable meaning of art and for many people a decisive meaning.

Tone is a way of building in us a conviction. Goldsmith's little poem is, I think, at first—and maybe at last—convincing. Faulkner's story "The Bear," as I said, gives me a very powerful shift of parts to a whole which I called "illumination." I am "convinced." Now, I happen to be attracted to the conviction that all is essentially one, that things will go on though in other shapes and manners. Yet I can be convinced of other views, too. I can feel in Fra Angelico's Virgin a form of revelation, quite a different view of the world from Faulkner's. This means, I suppose, that I have no center, no intellectual stability myself, puts me into the class of chameleon. I would not, however, want to say all art that did not agree with my view of things was bad art. A little "chameleonism" seems to me good. To react like a chameleon may imply that the truth of the conviction one is led to is less important than the artistic convincingness of the art: one cannot be equally convinced of one view today and another one tomorrow without casting some doubt on one's "believing" either and some doubt on the external reliability of either. The Greeks, so some doctors say, played tragedy in the morning and comedy in the afternoon, and at some time in the fifth century it was habitual for a dramatist to present a three-part tragedy immediately followed by a more or less comic "satyr play." Shakespeare put comic scenes in tragedies; he made Hamlet take on something the tone of Goldsmith in the gravedigger scene that precedes the final actions of the tragedy. I do not see how we can avoid saying Shakespeare was a chameleon and expected his audience to be. It is a fact that we can, within limits, shift our attitudes very quickly, and indeed want to. Few concerts are arranged to present music all of the same tone for fear monotony would set in; an exhibition of an artist who does the same thing over and over is a bore. We want variety of all sorts; the capacity of the human psyche for sexual excitement has limits; the mechanism reaches fatigue.

These instances suggest that art need not mean any one opinion, need not keep saying the same thing, though in different ways. If this makes doubtful the necessary verity of art, it does not, contrariwise, make doubtful the necessity of being *about* something or the necessity of its being convincing.

If we be convinced by the tone, order, logic, and internal consistency of a piece of art, we are, I think, inclined to feel the view of things it presents is possible. Aristotle, as I have mentioned before, felt that probability was more important than possibility. The two may approach one another very closely, however, for a good ghost story will leave its traces on our nerves, and we might be quite hesitant about darkness and odd creaks in the house after reading one. We can be "kidded" into believing fantasy not so much probable as possible. A great deal of art, however, deals with things that purport to be real; the artist takes a view of them and convinces us of his view; we tend to grant not only the seeming probability but the actual possibility. Some people, of course, are so sure of one position that they immediately refuse the chance of likelihood to anything that disagrees with their position. Many of us, however, live in a state of relative doubt, with sufficient humility to hear this position or that or the other. Thus the artist's point of view which he manages to make convincing to us we may consider wisdom. And wisdom is a possible external meaning of art. Wisdom need not come directly, for one can write a wise book that makes no outright statement. It comes rather in the way our feelings and attitudes are affected; it comes from seeing new relationships; it comes from our stretching our imaginations, our relative capacity to put together things we never before allied. Here the metaphorical and paradoxical habits of poetry serve to enliven and enlarge our minds by enlarging our view of things. What we call "insight" is a small flash of this sort of enlarged perception.

Let me use here one of my favorite pictures, "The Three Graces" by Rubens (Figure 9). It uses, with false imitation of course, a classical subject; the ladies are rather overclothed in flesh, so that, I find, women are enraged by it and men tend to giggle, forgetting they can be made to "love" such objects; there is a false modesty of wisps of gauze drawing attention to areas the gauze ought to hide; the surrounding "nature" is pretty theatrical—it is, on the face of it, a silly picture. Yet I find a kind of vitality in all that flesh, a delight in it, not an inducement to lust but rather a pure feeling for the living quality of it. Against all first prejudices toward the Rubens "Percheron" there rises this new insight of the being of flesh. It is in this way one learns by art; it is in this way comprehension comes.

The art which is about something, then, which draws on our deep and widespread feelings, cannot easily misuse and contradict them; it must maintain some sort of possible logic in order to reach probability; it must have, in another word, some sort of credibility. If it uses credibility with intelligence, we can regard the art as meaning wisdom.

There is in practice, however, some danger here, for in order to achieve credibility the art may become so average, so conventional that we are uninterested. There comes to be no question in our minds, no uncertainty;

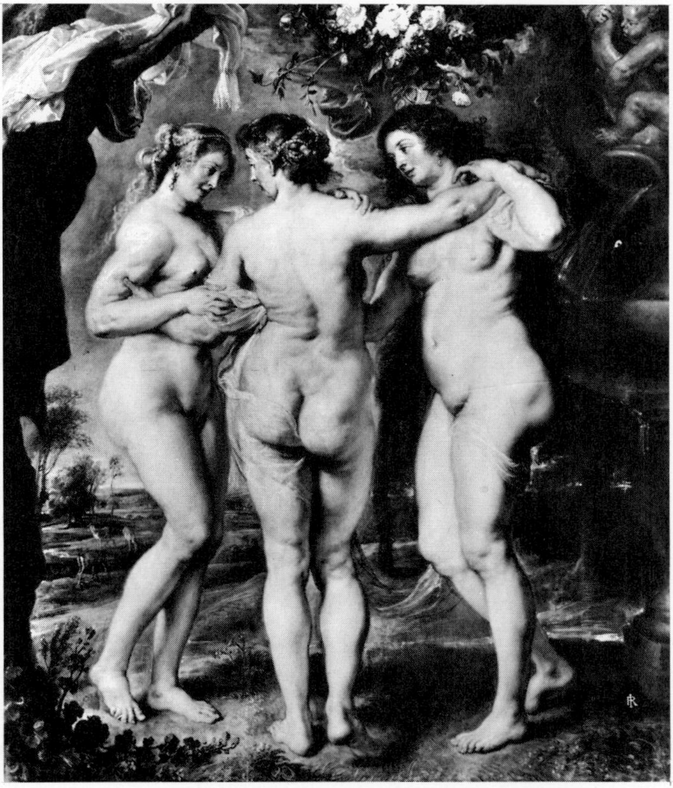

FIGURE 9. "The Three Graces" by Peter Paul Rubens, Prado Museum, Madrid. Photograph courtesy of Fratelli Alinari

we "cannot care less," we say; "the old corn," we say. Thus art tends to be in some degree offbeat, iconoclastic, especially the comic art. In a period of experimentation and reassessment of values, such as the recent period of our Western civilization, iconoclasm of all sorts has run to extravagance. This has been fun, stimulating, shocking; it is, however, hard to take most sculpture made of odds and ends seriously; even Picasso's set of figures composed of pieces of wood and picture frames and cast in bronze affects me chiefly as a good laugh, but then Picasso hasn't been, since his "blue period," altogether serious in intent anyhow, except for the time of the black and white "Guernica." Yet artists tend to be people with decided views and with a power of relating aspects of life; the result is often a conviction different from the common. We may not wish to follow, for many of us are frightened of the extreme and extraordinary, but we recognize a possible wisdom in the iconoclastic.

It is by some such way as this that art becomes educative. We do not act like Shakespeare's good characters; we may sometimes act like his villains; but the reading of Shakespeare will reassort our acceptances, our values, our attitudes, make us doubt, jar us from some comfortable conformities—even now, even after almost four hundred years. A play like Beckett's *Waiting for Godot*, a message play meant to show that we are in a tough world and can expect no help, may make us reassess our faiths and may even, through the warm brotherhood between the two main characters which it exhibits and which really makes the play "go," persuade us of the value of our relations with our fellows. Art, then, does not educate by outright statement—philosophy should be expected to use the outright statement—but by the new attitudes it breeds out of our old ones. I suspect its main value is sympathy, an understanding of how evil comes up to mistaken man. It is this increase of understanding through our reshaped attitudes that I think the chief revelation of art.

There is a converse here, of course: art may very well mislead us. What we mean by the cheap and the sentimental is that art which we think wants to persuade us that what we regard as evil is good. We can be weakened as well as strengthened by art. The piece of art that persuades us it is all right to do sloppy things, that this illogical attitude is right because everybody has it, that the way to live is the way the people in television commercials live—all the "cute" and the artificial and the stale—may be corrupting of genuine thought and genuine feeling. I think it impossible to maintain that art may educate wisely without admitting art may corrupt.

The educative meaning of art is inescapable; we cannot be made to feel deeply about anything and to feel in an orderly way without its leaving some sort of memory in our brains. I suspect details, pictorial effects, all that we first notice in stories and pictures and music, may vanish from memory before the attitudes generated in us; we can say, "Yes, a gay book" or "a bleak picture," without being able to name a character or quite formulate a memory of the shapes in the picture. It is often only what art has carved into our attitudes that remains to jump into life.

Art is about something; it makes us feel about its subject matter; it may make us think about its subject matter; it leads us to views of the world; it educates us. Does it speak "truth"?—or, preferably, is truth one of its possible meanings? It is easy to say "Yes" and easy to say "No," for the question of Pontius Pilate—"What is truth?"—is not an easy one to answer.

That a particular statement is true or not is discoverable, perhaps. "If you kick a rock, you'll hurt your toe" you can verify by trying. This sort of thing the scientist is inclined to call "fact"; though he deals with generalities—"a" pinch of salt, not this particular pinch of salt—and often with hypotheses—that light always travels at a given rate—he is likely to take these as givens, as facts, and leave truth as a word for something else. The philosopher tends to talk about "truth"; unfortunately, philosophers do not agree; each seems to erect a system, no doubt internally consistent, based on a premise. There are, however, various premises—*"Cogito, ergo sum"* for one—and so far as I can discover, the premise is a matter of choice. The same wriggling and protean quality inhabits the "great truths," the "eternal verities." These have the additional disadvantage that so few people seem to act upon them: "the love of money is the root of all evil," "love thy neighbor as thyself," "power corrupts," and so on. There is hardly a "truth" that is not arguable, though there are some we all say we accept. If arguable, then not "truth."

What does the artist do with truth? There is a famous poem by Lovelace that goes in part:

Stone walls do not a prison make,
Nor iron bars a cage:
Minds innocent and quiet take
That for an hermitage. . . .[3]

It sounds true. Would you be surprised if Mr. Lovelace, finding the prison door unlocked, walked out? Would his walking out make his poem nonsense? He has taken our customary opinion of prisons, that they limit our freedom, and shown us that true liberty is not where we are but how we are in spirit. Does it pass from poetic probability into realistic possibility? Does it matter whether it does or not?

I think I can suggest that it matters whether it be at all "reasonable." We can think of people who might feel fine in prison. Suppose Lovelace had written something that said "Prison is the freest place in the world: you have no obligation except to get out." Would this be equally "reasonable" and "true" or just a "wisecrack"? Suppose he had written, "No man is free in prison." Equally reasonable and true? You will easily see that the problem is semantic: what does "free" mean? Yet we get a statement that we can understand from Lovelace's poem, and it makes sense.

It is not such use of truth that is essentially the artist's, however. We know the great truths before we come to art, like as not, and their statement is not likely to stir us. What the artist does is to make us feel how they come up to particular characters out of particular situations, how general characteristics shine from *this* face or *this* place. The artist makes us see the sights, the action, and arouses the feelings accordant and consequent. In literature the whole process of a story or play may often be thought of as a particular case of a general idea; so *Macbeth* does not say so much that murderous ambition is bad—this we knew—as the process of its arising, acting, and reaching its end in this particular case. We can say, then, the play "means" ambition was bad in this case. Whatever we think of ambition in general, Shakespeare will have persuaded most of us that in this case it was bad. Forever after we shall have to count this example. This is a meaning. Do you wish to generalize from here? It is not regarded as good logic to generalize from one example, yet this, I think, is what we in fact do. We do not do it directly, though. We do not say, "Evil women are like Lady Macbeth." We see a real person with what we take to be Lady Macbeth's characteristics, and we say, "Ah! Lady Macbeth!" Thus Lady Macbeth is not typical to us until we make her so by application to another particular case. We may even say of a country club we don't like, "The place seems to be full of Lady Macbeths."

Thus, though the play does not as experience mean the general "truth"—"murderous ambition comes to a bad end" or "murder will out"—but uses our previous attitudes toward it to frame a new example, we do later in one way or another make the play and its characters types. It is in this way the play speaks "truth" and in this way that it gives knowledge.

We would feel neither as meaning if Macbeth and his lady were more odd and individualistic and extravagant. If we add up the characteristics Macbeth has, we will find the list is not very long. We say we "know" Macbeth; what we know is very little of him, not his taste in food, how he collects rents, how he leads soldiers, how he treated—or treats—his mother, and so on. I am not sure I could extrapolate from what Shakespeare has given me to these other characteristics. Yet I "know" Macbeth, what is essential to his situation and his story. This is the "truth" we can use as typical. Hamlet has always been to me a man with too many characteristics; he does so many things so well—except make up his mind, perhaps. It is interesting that so much has been written trying to settle what his character is, what "explains" him. This very uncertainty may, of course, have helped to make his play fascinating and disturbing, but it makes it very hard to find what the play "says."

The thing we can use as typical, then, is likely to be in its own way simplified in the beginning. Thus we can use it; thus it may seem to us "true," not of its own case only but of others as well. It is hard to say whether this sort of meaning is necessary for good art, for there have been many pieces of art whose fame has relied on their "quotability," and they are likely to have been works done by famous artists and valuable for other qualities as well. I suppose we have all read stories which seem to us to present things we could quote or use as typical cases; we have realized, though, that they were not widely enough known for a reference to them to come clear to many others. Their fame or lack of it grows in part by chance. It is, then, impossible to judge the critical necessity of typicality, yet I think it fair to say that the property is likely to be one we admire and find a meaning in.

This may seem a very haphazard way to treat such an important subject as Truth. I have suggested art may seem possible, that is, reliable as guide for actual people and events. I have suggested it may seem like wisdom, a word, I take it, for a more comprehensive and considered reliability than the possible. I have suggested that we can use art to describe cases from life, and perhaps we can use it to predict: when we say "Lady Macbeth" about a person, we are inclined to predict a bad end for her. And behind all these I have suggested the artist must use our reaction to generally known truths, for it is only out of these he can make impressive art. Yet I know a doubt gnaws: that what art seems to say may have a sanction greater than the artist's opinion and greater than guess. For art is revelatory.

What is it that we would want "truth" to be? It cannot be "the thing" itself; it must be a statement about the thing. A statement is not natural and objective; it is man-made and hence subjective to that degree. We want it to be the best that human minds can do. What would the best be? I think some characteristics we would insist on would be, so far as possible, "all-inclusive," "internally consistent"—that is, "logical"—and "applicable." The scientists insist truth means "predictability," and for that I use this last word, "applicable." Fiction and pictures tend to deal with particulars; some poetry puts itself in the generalizing, philosophical class: "Life is real! life is earnest!" or "We are such stuff as dreams are made on," which comes from a character in a play, of course; some religious icons may be regarded as general, I suppose—Buddhas, for instance—a kind of concentration in one image of a theory of life. Can art be all-inclusive in the way science feels it can? Again one reaches the question of how far one wishes to generalize from a single example. Can it be internally consistent? I suggest here one says, "It must," and indeed it often seems to be. Can it be applicable? Now I come once more to a question of individual choice. If we want to apply it, we can, but whether it will be reliable is another sort of question altogether, for art does not deal with inanimate objects but with human life. Though I have suggested people are pretty much alike, they are also diverse and different. We cannot say that being scared by a dog when young will leave an ineradicable fear of dogs; the best we can say is that it is likely. This is indeed as far as Aristotle can be taken to have gone when he insisted art was more truthful than history: history dealt with an example, art shows the likelihood—"most commonly"—which seems likely to an audience of many people because it is the mean of their diverse experience. It is only so far as this sort of statistical opinion that art's reliability can be expected to go.

And yet this may be the best we can do anyhow. The relativistic truth of art may be the greatest truth we can reach. The truth of art has the great advantage over philosophy that it shows not only the statement—"power corrupts"—but the very "feel" of the way power corrupts. One may learn more of the general statement this way than by any philosophic statement—unless the philosopher become a fabricator of fiction.

It is in this way, finally, that I think one can suggest the truth of art and the meaning art has as truth. The parables of Jesus are pieces of fiction; if you are a Christian believer, their truth is sanctioned by your faith that Jesus was divine; if you are not a Christian believer, the parables have no more sanction than other pieces of fiction. They were designed for the moral truth, like Aesop's fables. Most pieces of art, I think it can be said fairly, are not primarily so designed, yet whether designed for truth or not, truth of the parable may emerge, and it is such meaning we may find and may value in art.

Truth, knowledge, wisdom, conviction, revelation—these are possible external meanings of art. They are much alike; they come from our tendency to find use in things. I could suggest that it is only a Puritan kind of temperament that would feel things must be useful, but it is not only Puritans or people like them in other civilizations who have found truth in art. Some men never have their sexual desires satisfied; some men never have their desire for a sense of personal importance satisfied; some men never have their desire for knowing "how things really are" satisfied. This desire for knowledge Plato said was the last thing men would give up—though his whole theory went to show that the great majority of people must remain ignorant. I have as little explanation of our desire for knowledge as of our desire for order. I suppose the two to be somewhat allied, both deriving from those unanswered questions with which we find ourselves living. Art seems to satisfy both needs, and thus gives a profound meaning and a profound usefulness. If a diabolic voice whispers, "But is it Art?", I can only advise you to close your ears to the voice. Perhaps after the internal meanings of the experience of art, its stimulation and ordering of our psyches, are done with and their emotions have faded, we do naturally turn to some comparison of that experience with our ongoing view of life as we lead it; out of that comparison we may reach some new judgment how men act; out of it we may learn. And we may accept or reject a piece of art in this later contemplation by our judgment of its "truth."

CHAPTER 7

The Social Setting of Art

THROUGHOUT what has gone before, the properties of art per se and the several kinds of meaning one may find in it, there has run, I hope, an assumption that art takes place in a society. Society feeds the artist, and his audience is a part of a society which his art in turn feeds. His setting explains him in good measure; in good measure his effect on his setting and on those who come after judges him.

The Pueblo Indian bowl through its maker was a product of its tribe. The place it took in that tribe was one of usefulness but also one of pleasure, for it was made to be nice to look at. The Kutenai animal story was a delight to its listeners, but it made some criticism of its society; in its way it set out to improve. The slab of slate with two spirals on it and the story the old Australian told by it, which I mentioned at the very opening of this disquisition, had, however, another sort of place. The story was, we will say, the story of the tribe's origin and journeying, how it "got here," a creation story, a settling story, like Genesis. In the story would be gods and heroes, but also "the people," the tribe. Other tales would speak of the acts of heroes after the tribe had settled or had found its central home. Perhaps the most ancient of the heroic tales or epics that we have is that of Gilgamesh, a Mesopotamian hero; he journeyed across the sea of death to find Utnapishtim, whom the gods had, like Noah, told how to survive the flood and who had then been rewarded by that immortality which Gilgamesh sought him to find; Gilgamesh found him but could not win immortality; as a consolation prize he was shown the way to the rose of perpetual youth, only to have the rose stolen by a snake. This was a heroic story with a clear philosophic scheme; the philosophic scheme, however, explains "what happened in history."

The service of these hereditary tales is pretty clear: as the old Australian told his story, his listeners were given a sense of belonging, a sense of place in the world, a sense of brotherhood. For much of the year they were separate nomadic families; now they found the assurance of others, of their permanence, of their heritage. Perhaps nothing could make them feel their social cohesiveness as such tales did. All over the world such stories are found, one of the most remarkable the Polynesian history of thirty-five hundred years of travel from India to Hawaii, a history that the scholars find no reason to believe anything but largely right.

Mythologists fascinated by such stories believe them the great and basic kinds of literary art. Yet European civilization now finds itself largely cut off from them. The Homeric tales, the old stories like *Beowulf,* the poetry like the *Edda,* and the tales of Cuchulain in Ireland and Arthur in England—the last told more by Frenchmen and Germans than by Englishmen—are no longer taken to be the histories of European peoples. Such roots do not quite hold. And uprooting them, of course, was the Christian attempt to control loyalty, to impose across culture the transplant of Jewish heroes and Jewish history. When Europe came out of Christian internationalism into national states, it was too late to restore the vitality of the old stories. King Arthur in Malory's hands has not become the cultural base of England, and Charlemagne and Roland fared only a little better for the French. It is interesting that Shakespeare tried to give a background to Englishmen, quite consciously expressed in *Henry V;* but scientific historians were already at work, and his plays (though I suppose many Englishmen learned what history they knew from them) never reached the sanctity of legend. Without a national heroic legend we cannot now invent one. In a sense, Magna Carta is the creation story for Englishmen and the Constitution for Americans. We have tried to write the heroic song of Lincoln, but I think we know too much to be able to do it. We get as far as folk songs about Jim Henry and Casey Jones and half-remembered stories of Daniel Boone and Davy Crockett—and Jesse James. I suppose the greatest folk hero of my time may be John L. Lewis, but I do not believe one can write an epic about him. Can the American Negro make a heroic legend about Martin Luther King? The confines of reality do not allow the enlargement of epic myth. Even the Fourth of July oration is over, and the parade is no more the continuation of a sense of heritage than the Christmas parade of Macy's, and not likely to be so much fun. One of the old and central positions of art, if tribal and heroic tales be such, is no longer possible for us, and this place of heritage art can no longer take.

Tribal history may have spoken of gods and the deeds of gods, and what it said may have been developed as an explanation of ritual, but it was not religious. Religion and its rituals grew from something else and were otherwise directed. They grew from the place of man in nature, in the great cycle of the seasons, and from man's need of nature's fertility. Their origin is hard to imagine, but we are most of us superstitious in some way or another—I always put on my right shoe before my left, for instance. Superstition is an avoidance: do this and evil will not fall. Magic is positive: do this and things will happen. Tribal ceremony, ritual performance, grew from magic, by jumps we can no longer re-create. It was not directed at the audience but at the powers of nature; our only modern counterpart of tribal ceremony is, perhaps, the Roman Mass, directed at a deity with the audience as implied participants.

Tribal people feel and felt themselves parts of nature and their duty to be the assistance of nature; this is not placation, not preaching, but help. The picture of isolated, fear-filled man I think untrue of early times, and perhaps what makes Christians regard "savages" as merely superstitious is their failure to cringe, to abase themselves before their deities; gods and men are part of nature. The ancient tribal ceremony was not to keep the sun up when it was about to sink in winter but to assist it to sink so that it might properly rise in spring. The key word here, I think, is "properly." Nature must be helped to do what nature is meant to do, and the ceremony of assistance must be properly done, must be letter-perfect. The performance might turn out to be artistically "right," but the purpose was magical. The "best" must go into it, for what men felt to be best would have most power. Into this best would be poured the resources of the tribe, skill and time and goods: songs and music, hymns, chants, prayers, dances, masks and costumes, regalia of all sorts, chapels and temples, altars, effigies, and so on, for on the propriety of nature all life depends.

Among American Indians the most ceremonial are, perhaps, the Zuni, over half their year being devoted to "dances" of various sorts. The origin story of the Zuni tells of emergence from the earth and of later journey; partway, crossing a river, half the people were drowned and came to live in Kachina Lake, water spirits plainly, and to them all the dying go, to become "grandfathers," gods depersonalized and in a way inhuman. The ceremonies are largely the return of various Kachina to Zuni, and the stories of the many individual ones and of their activities are the myths of Zuni. Among these ceremonies the most impressive, I am told, is the one on the first night of the six-day ceremony in December, just before the solstice, when the Shalako gods appear.

The Shalako god is one of the water spirits, represented by a mask, here shown in a kiva, or chapel, in Zuni during the Shalako dances (Figure 10). The mask and costume, ten feet tall and held up on a pole and held out by hoops, with ropes inside so that the wearer can make the beak clack and the eyes move, have been set down here for a while beside the god's altar, and one of the two men who alternate carrying the mask is resting. The men who were to act Shalako—two for each of six masks—have spent a year learning the prayers, chants, hymns, dances, movements of the ceremony. Every new moon they have planted prayer sticks—which are wooden phallic symbols with feathers bound to them by cotton thread—each time with a prayer. They have now been through some days of sexual continence and some time of abstinence from food; they have been washed clean and purged by vomiting. The mask, which

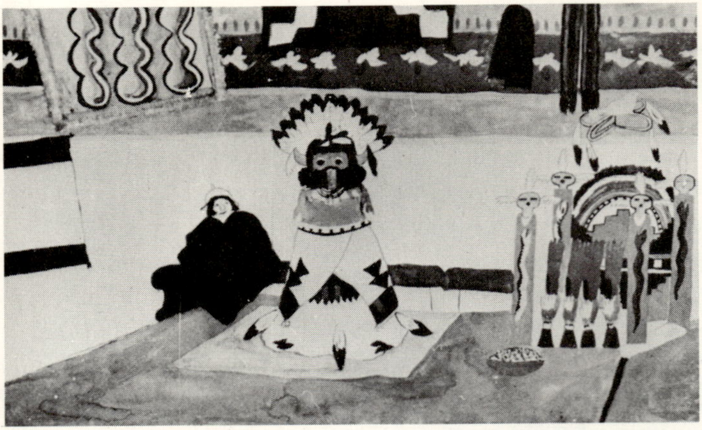

FIGURE 10. Shalako in Kiva from "Zuni Katcinas" by Ruth L. Bunzel, in *The 47th Annual Report* of the Bureau of American Ethnology, 1929–1930, Government Printing Office, Washington, D. C.

is a tribal possession, has been kept in its own shrine and ceremonially fed tobacco and food every day. It has been cleaned and repainted, the facial color turquoise blue. The costume has been made and readied. The kiva, up to sixty feet long and twelve feet high, with another room beyond windows so that more of the tribe may look on, has been built by the dancers and by the host, who has offered to pay for materials and for the decoration—all, really, a communal activity. The mask and costume have been ceremonially taken out from their shrine with appropriate prayers. The dancer has this afternoon put on the mask and by doing so has become, in a sense, this birdlike god. At dusk, with his fellows and preceded by Sayatasha, the most dignified of the council of gods, and his attendants, he has entered the village to the singing of hymns and to definite steps. He has paused at the door, planted seeds in the doorway, in boxes hung from the ceiling, and in small pits in the floor, praying for increase each time. He has walked the path of sacred meal—corn, shell, turquoise ground up together—to this spot. He has just now been greeted by his host, and at being asked why he has come and what he has done, has said that as a god living in the sacred lake he always wanted to come, that he has passed all the sacred springs where prayer sticks were planted, and that he wants his people to be happy, especially in their children. He has brought seeds of all sorts, for he wants his children to be healthy, to have fresh water, and to stand up firmly on their feet all year.

Presently the dancer will put on his costume and for two hours recite his long chant, telling in detail what he has done during the year. Then he will dance the rest of the night, alternating with his fellow dancer; singers, a drummer, a rattle-shaker will supply music, many songs varied in rhythm. The ten-foot bird will swoop and pause, turn, move from side to side, according to those who have seen him, with great delicacy and great power, with a sense of vitality building up, and the tribal spectators will sit spellbound in awe of this sense of power that is being danced into nature.

Tomorrow, after Sayatasha, the leader of the council of gods, has recited from a rooftop his morning chant (his *evening* chant was six hours long), the Shalako gods will leave the village, and after having gone away, will run. The young men will chase them, for catching one is a sign of good luck. The dancers then will be ceremonially cleansed of the divinity they assumed when they put on the mask, and the year's work will be over.

Let me put down the chant the man taking this position may recite as he plants his prayer sticks each month. The longer chants are like this in language and general shape.

This chant describes the making of prayer sticks or plume wands. "Making days," which you will read, means keeping the proper period of abstinence or taboo before a ceremony. This is the man speaking to the gods; trees, turkeys, cotton thread are all called father or mother, an intimate animist feeling about the world.

This many are the days
Since at the new year
For those who are our fathers
Ka-eto-we, teu-eto-we,
The days were made.
From all the wooded places;
Breaking off the young straight shoots
Of the male willow, female willow
In our hands we held them fast.
With them we gave our plume wands human form.
With the striped cloud wing
The one who is our father
Male turkey
We gave our plume wands human form
With the flesh of our mother
Cotton woman,
Even a poorly made cotton thread
With this four times encircling the plume wands
And tying it about their bodies
We finished our plume wands
Having finished our plume wands
And offering our fathers their plume wands
We made their days
Anxiously awaiting their days
We have passed their days
After a little while
Your masked clouds
Your rains we shall desire
We have given you plume wands
That with your waters
Your seeds

Your riches
Your long life
Your old age
You may bless us.
For this I have given you plume wands
To this end, my fathers
May our roads reach to dawn lake
May our roads be fulfilled
To where the road of our sun father goes
May our roads reach
May our roads be fulfilled
May we grow old
May we be blessed with life.[1]

This is ritual poetry. One can feel the rather stylized language, the repetitive patterns, and the order: we have done this, grant us increase. This is a man speaking to a god, but a man who is saying, "I have done the proper things. Now you do them in turn." When the gods, such as the Shalako, appear, they come to promise that requests will be granted. None of this is pleading, cringing, praying. It is formal and without feeling. There is a myth that formerly when they departed, the Shalako "took someone with them" to Kachina Lake, for this is a ceremony in December in the beginning of deathly winter, but such does not happen now. All gods, all kachinas, are ancestors, all bringers of rain, in a sense all fertility gods, *not* made in man's image, dangerous because coming from death, but happy, friendly, beneficent.

The emotion of the ceremony does not come from the human likeness of the gods, or from personal expressions of feeling, but from qualities in the rhythm, the imaginative design of costumes, the songs, the motions of the dances, the hypnotism, perhaps, of the ceremony. It is dramatic, in a way, surely, but it does not have issues, loves, hates, hopes, fears, rights, wrongs. It is not directed toward the audience so much as incantation of the power of nature: it dances the power of nature into being. It must be carried out properly, letter-perfect, and that perfection must add to its power. We say, of course, it cannot affect nature; the Zuni say it does. We can see, however, that what it does is to assure the community, to bind it together psychologically, to make every member a part of a successful and satisfactory whole.

The Zuni are a cohesive and peaceful people, and they see their gods as kindly. Elsewhere, in other lands, the anthropologists and mythologists say, there has been sacrifice to more violent gods by more violent and emotional people.

Other myths grow, as at Zuni, from man's need of fertility, from his place in the ecology of nature, from the cycles of the seasons. The great power of the world is fertile and feminine, and by this likeness and perhaps by the relation of the moon to the feminine menstrual cycle, the great divinity becomes the earth mother, the moon goddess. She has borne many names around the world: as mother, Rhea and Ge and Demeter and Hera and Cybele and Padma and Tiamat and Freya; as goddess, Ishtar and Astarte and Attis and Aphrodite and Persephone and Ariadne and Artemis and Isis and Sita and Helen and even local names like Brynhild and Calypso and Circe and Penelope and once, perhaps, Guinevere. The great ceremony was her marriage, for she needed annual impregnation, and annually in spring her human counterpart or priestess was given a mate. Her secret or public conjunction with her "King" was an example to nature to conceive and to bear. While the agricultural year waxed, the King was strong; when it waned into fall, his power left him, and he must die. Thus, it is said, came the ceremony of sacrifice, of the "dying god," the "lover" remembered in the stories of Tammuz and Adonis and Tithonus and Osiris.

We cannot get back to the ceremonies of prehistoric days; the fabrics are rotted away, the songs and dances forgotten. There are a few idols of the goddess, from as far back as twenty-five thousand years ago, the fat "Venuses" of Europe; there are many little "dolls" of animals to be put into the fields to encourage fertility; and the seals in clay or stone of Mesopotamia and Crete show the mother goddess. We can imagine the songs and dances of celebration of the sacred marriage and imagine some tension and awe at a public conjunction, which led inevitably to the happy obscene joke, and led further, as remnants show in Ramadan of the Near East and the faschings of Dresden or the Mardi Gras of Christian lands, to general sexual indulgence. All was broken down into relaxation and release and to joy and confidence and assurance; the goddess had been properly married, and nature was freed to act. Out of such ceremonies came, by long and unknown steps, but bearing something of its heritage, the classical comedy of Aristophanes. Indeed, even in the very different Zuni at certain ceremonies the Kokoshi appear, sacred spirits who crack vulgar and obscene jokes and do clown tricks.

The relaxation and assurance of the spring ceremony are clear. The winter ceremony of the King's death, however, was more moving, as the sight of death is more enthralling and more final than the sight of copulation. One can try, I think, to imagine the psychology of sacrifice: the preparation, dressing up and bringing in the victim, songs, no doubt, the entrance of a priest and a chant by him, the placing of the victim, some other chant or prayer, suddenly the blows of death, and the burst of what the Greeks called the threnos, the song of lamentation at the year's death. Emotionally, this would be the looming of horror, the building up of it, the spasm of the death blow, the release into sorrowful song, and then the return to "reality" again, the audience shaken still, perhaps, but assured that nature had been, not propitiated, but made to act and that now the world was properly ordered and would go on.

There were, of course, ceremonies of animal sacrifice, too, propitiatory ceremonies, ceremonies to ward off evil, ceremonies to placate the dead. Not all people saw the dead as "grandfathers"; the dead might be vengeful; the Greeks called them "Keres," sometimes pictured them as wizened fairies, and fancied that in a way they fastened themselves on their descendants and became what are mistakenly translated as "fates." In Egypt a great deal of the art we know was devoted to burial, to the journeying of the soul, or Ka, to the underworld of Osiris; neither Babylonians nor Greeks nor Hindus nor Chinese, in spite of their ancestor worship, so poured their energies into tombs. Like the ceremonies of placating and so keeping off the dead was the ceremony in which the evils of a society were put on one animal or man who was sent out to exile or to death. The Jews used a goat, the scapegoat; the Greeks a man, stranger or criminal, who was called a "pharmakos" and his ceremony a purging, or "catharsis." These two have given words to our medical vocabulary, and the second, catharsis, Aristotle took for the final effect of tragedy. The placatory ceremonies, the ceremonies of avoidance, had the effect, like the fertility ceremonies, of bringing society together and of giving it assurance, a very profound purging of fear and psychologic upset.

When men with their sun gods took over from matriarchal women with their moon goddesses, when, in effect, Zeus took over from Rhea and mythically raped various local goddesses or made them his children, it was clear that the annual King could no longer be killed: the King ruled, if he could, for life, and if the ceremony of fertility of the women must be continued, animals must be substituted for men. The Aegean lands invented now one great deity of vegetation: Dionysus, with choruses of frenzied women and of men with horsetails and erect phalli, the satyrs. He came from the Near East, perhaps, certainly fairly late into Greece. He became an annual deity, born at Eleusis, thriving all over Greece, killed as a bull in Crete and eaten raw by priests seeking the remnants of his vitality, and buried at Delphi, where he shared the year with the sun god Apollo. In Ikaria, Dionysus was annually killed as a goat; from that town came Thespis, the reputed father of Greek drama, and the word tragedy, or "goat song," can be derived as well as from anything from the Ikarian song of lamentation at the goat's annual death. With the male gods, however, something had gone of the old impressiveness and the old social cohesion. Only Dionysus seemed to keep his power but rather as fun for the men and frenzy for the women than as affecting nature's acts.

The drama of Greece was begun, so far as we know, at Athens, the great cosmopolitan city of the sixth century, and it was devoted to Dionysus, the god of fertility, grain and cattle and wine. As we have it in Aeschylus, from some way along in the fifth century, it was put on the stage by the city, a public performance. This was no longer a song to the gods nor a dancing of vitality into the gods, no longer an assistance *to* the gods, but a performance for the enjoyment and instruction of the people. Yet if one looks at Aeschylus' *Agamemnon*, one can see the ritual shape, I think. It is a year-king story in origin, perhaps, transformed into a domestic triangle and enlarged therefrom by its social philosophy of justice. It has, however, a remnant of one great characteristic of ritual: the act must be done and is not motivated or explained. So in *Agamemnon* the first speeches and choruses, however joyfully they begin, all end in fear of doom, "May all yet be well!" We feel a doom will come, but we do not know why or by what. This foreboding rises to the unmatchable scene of Cassandra divining past and coming bloodshed, a moment's pause, then the three great cries of Agamemnon's death. Then Clytemnestra appears to boast of her deed, to sing the threnos with the chorus: only then, afterward, does she explain her action. After Aegisthus speaks his triumph and a little flurry we come to the hope of peace. This seems to me to have a good deal of the ritual feeling, humanized and personalized as it is, and I think it very possible that the Athenian audience, which seems, from what little record we have, to have been moved as one might be at a bullfight at such ceremonies as the annual killing of a bull, might well have transferred the curve of psychic response the ritual evoked over to such a play as *Agamemnon* and its sequel, the *Choephoroi*, or to *Oedipus the King*. This last combines, indeed, the year-king ceremony, though that much transformed, and the pharmakos ceremony, clearer, but its emphasis is more on the pharmakos than on the purging. We have no record of the reaction of the Athenian audience, of course; we have so few of the plays that we cannot from their winning or not winning the prize tell what the audience liked better or worse than the plays we have and why. Yet tragedy bears,

I think, always this sense of horror, this act necessarily and inescapably done, and the release from it into assurance the world runs properly. This assurance, in Zuni and in Greece, was a social assurance and the purpose of ceremony.

The Greek drama—and there is very little drama of anything like its quality in the rest of the world—had, however, in the main crossed from the ritual direction toward the gods to the modern direction toward the audience. Euripides especially began to make his drama depend upon motive, on "why do" rather than on "do." Medea debates the slaughter of her children; Theseus' motivated and mistaken anger calls down disaster on Hippolytus. This was not yet modern in emphasis, of course, but it had begun to pass from the inescapable ritual to the debatable mistake, and Aristotle, hunting for a logical reason why the king must fall, did not see the ritual reason but invented what came to be known as the "tragic flaw." The effect is not the assistance of nature and the conclusion into assurance the world will properly run, but the inculcation of morality.

Something of the same shift can be found in the other arts of Greece, from the stiff early sculpture of 600 B.C. through its gradual humanizing until in Periclean times the statues, such few as we have of them, tended to assume a calm, confident, outward look over an attractively vigorous body. Perhaps the sixth-century maidens of the Acropolis with their odd smile retained some feel of divinity, and there are records that the great statues of Athena and Zeus that Phidias made held some power of awe; but such a statue as this of the slain soldier Kroisos expresses not divinity but healthy humanity (Figure 11), and when we get to the end of the fifth century, to the famous Victory fastening her sandal, one can tell by

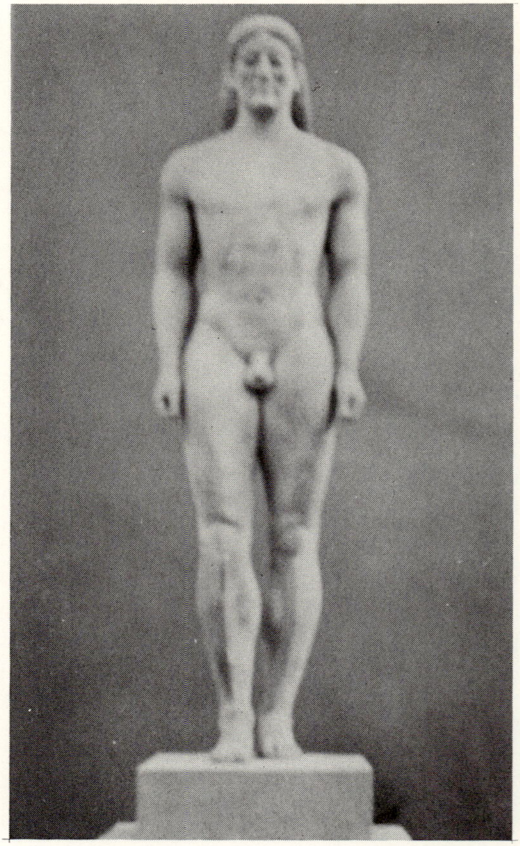

FIGURE 11. Kroisos from Anavyssos, National Museum, Athens

the pose and by the disclosures of the flesh that we are in no ritual climate, nor even in the national imperial climate of Pericles, but in one that wishes chiefly to present pleasant sights to the audience.

The humanist end of Greece is not far from our Western world today: man's place in nature is gone; the sense of the seasons as a necessary part of ecology is gone; and the close companionship of the gods is gone. Ritual as the activity done by the whole community to help nature can no longer take place; even the sense of the great temple being a city's center and sign of stability, such a sign as were the temples of Athens, Olympia, Bassae, Paestum, Selinunte, Segesta, cannot now be replaced by the Houses of Parliament, St. Paul's Cathedral, the Capitol, or the rebuilding of Pittsburgh.

Meanwhile, through the long interregnum of Christianity a further shift was made: art was devoted not to nature or the assistance of nature, but to a separate deity; it was not this life that must be ordered for this life's sake but this life for another, and if one found this life a vale of tears, one could retreat from society in expectation of a life after death. The appeal of the religion was to the individual; art was made by the community for devotion to the saints and the three parts of God, but it was not the community whose saving was thought of so much as the individual's sanctity. The Christians took over the major ritual times of year, but Jesus was born when he should have been killed and died when he should have been born. The Christian passion combines the dying god and the god's rebirth. One's eyes are on the sufferer, however, and his slayers are evil, so that one feels sorrow but not the inescapable quality of tragedy. Yet when believers feel "he died for us and we may now be saved," though this be individual and not tribal, some of the assurance of tribal ceremony is aroused, and in the resurrection tensions are relieved in joy. Perhaps this is melodrama, perhaps comedy, as Dante called it; for believers it is moving and in its own way purgative.

Christian visual art of many kinds, in many lands and in many centuries, has been sturdy, decorative, delicate, impressive. The churches became the centers of town life, and often a local saint was elevated to prominence among the legendary Jewish holy figures. Yet the tendency of the church was "universal," and universality was too large, vague, distant for the local group to feel a part of; during the great Christian centuries the people who went to the churches were not also the people who made up the government. As in Egypt and Persia, the tribal or civic unanimity was broken, and the Christian worshiper received not so much a sense of social cohesiveness and social assurance as assurance of his own final security.

There was no Christian tragedy. The saint who, like St. Theodore, was captured, burnt, his flesh torn from him, and yet sang hymns to the end aroused pity and tears but not terror, and he gave not social assurance for this life but individual assurance of a place in death. The death of Roland in the epic *Song of Roland* is sad but also happy. The death of Arthur is overwhelmingly sad, though brought on by his own incestuous sin, yet it brings no assurance, only a feeling that all worldly political and social struggle is futile before the necessary individual struggle for sanctity that the search for the Grail represents. After all, the sinner who has some good in him will finally be saved, and the utterly bad man must be hated and spurned; the shape of tragedy is not possible in the Christian cosmos. Nor can there be a social comedy of the Resurrection. The great Christian *Commedia* of Dante's is neither funny nor socially pointed; the old Aristophanic release and purgation are impossible.

Christian art was devotional and individual, and its social effect lay in its personal morality. And from that we have only hesitantly escaped.

The Renaissance tried to plunder the classical world; it thought that it restored the feeling by using the subjects: but too much had gone on to leap backward. I think an honest appraisal will show how false most of Renaissance art was, like the church fronts which imposed a kind of theatrical set piece on a building of a different shape. Of all the Italian painters after 1400, I am inclined to feel only Fra Angelico and Michelangelo stand up as maintaining integrity. The rest lost their logic in various attempts to impress, however impressive their technique turned out to be. There is no more saddening collection of "costume drama" than the Prado Museum in Madrid exhibits. Literature shows a like purpose, but from it a few names rise, the chief of all being Shakespeare, who has nowhere a second as close to him as the three great Athenian tragedians were to each other. (If there be any near second to Shakespeare between 1400 and 1600, it would be, I guess, Rabelais.)

Shakespeare's purposes were unlike the tribal or the Greek. Perhaps some of ritual feeling still held for Euripides; it was gone from Shakespeare. There is little feeling of man's participation in nature, though a good deal of reference to nature. There is, contrariwise, little feeling of a Christian sort; these are not devotional plays, and there is not, as even in the *Song of Roland,* a sense that heroism is rewarded in heaven. These are plays of this world; they are plays of motive, of error, moral plays.

The moral drama, that is, a drama in which the choices of the characters and our opinion of the characters depend upon their virtue or their vice, seems always to have to be one in which virtue must win. If the protagonist err, he is not good; where shall our sympathies lie? What do we want to have happen to him? Morally, he should be punished, and the play would not be tragedy but comedy. Thus there needs to be someone worse than the protagonist, a villain, to make him seem better and worth our sympathy. Clytemnestra, Orestes, Oedipus, Medea are not villains; we do not judge them morally but intellectually, if we judge at all; in the ritual drama before the Greek, no one could be judged, even intellectually, for the only force was the worshiped force, the nature of the world. In the moral drama of Shakespeare the villain often supplies the force; it is through him that the protagonist comes to err. Thus Richard II, Macbeth, Othello, Lear need the push of villainous opponents to bring them down. Even Antony needed the opposition of Octavius, who is not exactly villainous but certainly not good. *Hamlet* is an odd play, for it is not Claudius who really pushes Hamlet to death—this opposition is a mere fight—and when Hamlet has, even in a roundabout way, killed Claudius, he has done his job, has not erred, and should survive. The villain makes it possible for us to be on the hero's side; the villain becomes an inescapable force, like nature in the ritual drama, and thus the moral tragedy may seem inevitable. We can now pity the hero, and as we do so, may transfer our attitude from pity, which is external to him, to join him, and, in the face of inevitability, feel Aristotle's terror. Just before the critical act arises the opposition of our wish and the moral law; though we may be on Othello's side against Iago, the moral law must win, Othello die—clearly the villain must also die—and we must acknowledge the propriety of this. This is, I think, the order of the moral tragedy of Shakespeare. It is not the ritual tragedy or even Greek tragedy: it is based on a different world and a different psyche. The mistakes of the moral drama are never mistakes we would make; we see around them from the beginning: we would not murder Duncan or disinherit Cordelia or disbelieve Desdemona. And yet deep down in us we cannot condemn, for we are but a subconscious step above these acts. Shakespeare evokes, I think, a sense of looming horror and brings us to that state where we do not want it but do want it; our evil wishes, lying dormant in our Freudian subconscious, are touched to life: Duncan must be murdered! Then, through our altered attitudes, we discover in the disaster of the hero that his acts and our wishes were evil; we are, in a sense, "psychiatrized," purged, cured, made whole, and come out to the world we know realizing it is right and good. Tragedy is not effective because the world is tragic but because tragedy cures us of evil, because it re-establishes the sanity of life, because it confirms us in our world.

This seems to me social in effect. This seems to me a value in literature. We can be no longer a tribe in fellowship undergoing an experience and coming out to tribal cohesiveness, but each of us, individually, can be brought into a realization of the sanity of the world we share. With other purposes and another psyche, Shakespeare—and very few other Europeans—manages a final effect not far from that of ritual.

The comedy of Aristophanes usually maintained some choral celebration of the birth of Dionysus or of a sacred marriage. It made more, perhaps, of the inevitable obscenity of spring ceremonies. To a conventional moral judgment obscenity is bad, and the mention of activities we mostly perform in private is taboo. It is not so easy to explain this as it seems; the taboo occurred before Christianity and occurs in many places in the world. The "dirty joke" relies upon our sexual repression; it breaks that down, releases us, makes us companions in recognizing our common humanity. I remember seeing the stage performance of Tennessee Williams' *A Streetcar Named Desire*, wherein at one moment his wife, Stella, emotionally returns to Stanley Kowalski; as she rushed into his arms, the Stanley of the performance I saw gave her a great big, resounding, affectionate slap on her rear; a titter arose from what I took to be all the married women in the audience; the titter rose until all the audience laughed in delight. The actors did not try to go on with their lines; they had built for this laugh and knew it would come every night. I think the scene destroyed a lot of falsity and made the audience more human and brotherly. This does not mean that every utterance of four-letter words from the stage is a curative thing; it does mean that the low-class joke properly used, even the sexual one as Aristophanes continually used it in *Lysistrata,* can purge some of our inhibitions in a psychologically effective way.

Most comedy, of course, depends upon showing up folly. As we can each of us be guilty of this, but are not being individually criticized by the actors on the stage (Aristophanes *did* name some of his political enemies), we can be purged of our folly by being made to laugh at the same folly in others. And this seems to me as socially moral as the purgation of tragedy, even though laughter is more momentary than horror and cannot sustain as long a buildup before it as horror can.

Thus the moral tragedy and the social comedy act through the individual but have a tendency to make us accept our world and to make us more cohesive. It is not the tribal effect, but it is a social effect of a kind after all, climbing back as it can across the rift of Christian individualism where there was neither comedy nor tragedy.

In a much smaller way even such a thing as the Pueblo bowl cannot avoid some moral effect. One of the ones previously looked at had a round, evenly curved outline; the attentive eye does not pause, as I suggested, so that the bowl presents no problem, no vitality; it is average, undistinguished. Another of the bowls straightened its curve a little, gave some suggestion of vitality; I think by empathy this "perks up" the personality and so in this way enters the area of morality. So the verbal and visual vitality in an author's style may "perk us up," vitalize us. One can argue whether this be good or bad, but that it enters, however subtly, this moral area seems to me inescapable.

We cannot remain unaffected by anything that absorbs us and stirs us. As I have suggested, even a ghost story will leave traces on our responses; I can reawaken the eerie feeling, the doubt about the world's common-sense reality, that certain ghost stories long ago gave me. Not all that is so done to us is good in my morality; we may be weakened as well as strengthened. The arguments among parent groups about the effects of movies and television and comics are not idle arguments, I'm afraid, as Plato saw about the stories Athenian nurses told their children. No one knows the long-range effect of the mass commercial art American children are exposed to; there can, I think, hardly avoid being some effect. We can argue that exposure to it and discovering its falsity is wholesome; growing out of it is a good thing that could not otherwise be managed—but do all grow out of it?

Indeed, art has as many dangers as virtues. Aristotle mentioned with scorn that in his time there were serious plays in which things turned out happily, to please the wishes of the audience. We have had, since the last century put them on with a musical background, a name for such plays, melodrama. The foremost example for us now is, I suppose, the Western, but Shakespeare was not immune, for *A Winter's Tale* and *All's Well That Ends Well* among others can be held melodramatic, and the playwrights around him and after him tried to please by melodramatic means. The mark of melodrama is the unlikely action, the unprepared renewal, the extravagant tension. The town marshal strides out into the town square, alone and exposed, and a dozen armed bad men lurk around that square, hidden and ready to shoot him; the good girl idiotically tries to track down the murderer by going unarmed to his hideout. Though town marshals who were so stupidly heroic would have shirked their duty by dying, we accept the incredibility of the Western and can be delighted by the geometric decorations of its style, as we can by the game of the crime story. It is the melodrama that purports to be serious and that may enthrall us into believing such falsity possible that brings on melodrama its opprobrium. Again we must put Aristotle's caution on "possibility." We cannot ask an author to limit himself to statistical chances, of course; there is a chance that a scorned wife would be saved and hidden for twenty years and then presented to her husband as a statue, and we cannot ask that art be not extraordinary, for the ordinary would be useless to us, but the chance of the happy ending in *A Winter's Tale* seems pretty small. If we feel it improbable, our attitudes toward the world are not altered, and we can accept the melodrama of the play as a sort of genial joke. Were Shakespeare false enough to make us accept the only very slightly possible as probable, so that we could feel the world *was* like this, we would, I think, be damaged. We would do better to believe the world was not like this; we would be stronger and more honest.

Integrity, then, which is a moral value, puts its finger on melodrama.

The sentimental and the melodramatic are brothers in sin; they ask of us responses we are fools to grant. The sentimental is a begging for feeling; if we do not fall for it, as when we believe the melodramatic improbable, we may not be damaged, I suppose, only scornful. If we allow the sentimental, the false hope, the tear for the undeserved, the wish we should know cannot be granted to dominate us, we are by so much diminishing the veracity of our responses and of our characters. Where tragedy, by showing our unresolved wishes for evil are indeed evil, purges us, melodrama either ennobles such wishes or avoids bringing them into the light at all. Sydney Carton's sacrifice in *A Tale of Two Cities* is perhaps possible —though to rely on good men making such sacrifices would be foolhardy—but that he should accept it gladly seems to me some degradation of *his* character and some degradation of ours in allowing ourselves to be complacent in accepting it.

There is no hard and fast rule to define melodrama and sentimentalism, for they depend upon our view of what is possible, right, probable, "real." Here we reach the need of defining the "truth" about the way the world "really" goes, a definition so elusive that we frequently must leave decision to choice. Yet the purposely melodramatic and the purposely sentimental can be spotted pretty easily by a little comparison with the world as most of us see it. The sentimental and melodramatic may not touch us; they may not, then, be immoral in effect; but their positive value is nil, and they miss the social responsibility that some people may feel one of the values of art.

Sentimentalism, I think, is not only an appeal to overkindly feelings; it may appeal to our false cynicisms as well. Consider a poem by T. S. Eliot, "Animula"—little soul.

> *"Issues from the hand of God, the simple soul"*
> *To a flat world of changing lights and noise,*
> *To light, dark, dry or damp, chilly or warm;*
> *Moving between the legs of tables and of chairs,*
> *Rising or falling, grasping at kisses and toys,*

Advancing boldly, sudden to take alarm,
Retreating to the corner of arm and knee,
Eager to be reassured, taking pleasure
In the fragrant brilliance of the Christmas tree,
Pleasure in the wind, the sunlight and the sea;
Studies the sunlit pattern on the floor
And running stags around a silver tray;
Confounds the actual and the fanciful,
Content with playing-cards and kings and queens,
What the fairies do and what the servants say.
The heavy burden of the growing soul
Perplexes and offends more, day by day;
Week by week, offends and perplexes more
With the imperatives of "is and seems"
And may and may not, desire and control.
The pain of living and the drug of dreams
Curl up the small soul in the window seat
Behind the Encyclopedia Britannica.
Issues from the hand of time the simple soul
Irresolute and selfish, misshapen, lame,
Unable to fare forward or retreat,
Fearing the warm reality, the offered good,
Denying the importunity of the blood,
Shadow of its own shadows, specter in its own gloom,
Leaving disordered papers in a dusty room;
Living first in the silence after the viaticum.

Pray for Guiterriez, avid of speed and power,
For Boudin, blown to pieces,
For this one who made a great fortune,
And that one who went in his own way.
Pray for Floret, by the boarhound slain between the yew trees,
Pray for us now and at the hour of our birth.[2]

The poem is well organized in its first section on the divisions of "issues . . . the . . . soul," and the final section of sudden emotion about prayer for the violent (Dante's "lost, violent souls" again) gives a sounding contrast. Yet what is the poem about? It is not easy to decide whether the little soul is a particular child or is Eliot or is a modern child or is all of us; one is inclined to believe from the last line that it is all of us. At any rate, it is contemporary, and the names of the violent suggest they were long ago: the contrast, if there be one, seems to be our time and some romantic past time. What it asks us to feel is cynicism, a disgusted look at ourselves. This appeals to a good many people, I realize, but it seems to me a dishonest way to see mankind, and it is certainly not the way Eliot was, for he was a hardworking and very ambitious and productive person. The same kind of sentimentalism is, I am afraid, true of several of J. D. Salinger's stories, such as the tear asked for Seymour in "A Perfect Day for Bananafish." And I suspect that the major charge against *Waiting for Godot* will be the kind of tear for us all that Beckett's existentialism asks and hardly deserves.

The charge against the appeal to easy and unresolved feelings is the charge of dishonesty. All artists of any moment want to be accepted; most wish to make money. Artists are not dishonest because they trade their talent for the means to live. I suppose they are not dishonest if they do not know any better than to be sentimental, and a great many artists whom the critics may feel sentimental honestly believe in the genuine quality of their work. There are, however, artists who ought to know better, and the criterion by which we judge them unacceptable is the moral one of their failure to think harder, their failure to face up to the implications of their work, to the dilemmas of their work's organization. It is for this reason I have for long criticized Tolstoi's *Anna Karenina;* he found no way to end his heroine but to make her jump under a train; the solution is too easy, though suicides were fashionable literary devices of the time. Shall we weep for Anna? Is she worth the tear? This is the sort of thing I am suggesting as melodrama and dishonest and hence immoral. It tries to persuade us the world is not as the world is and as we had better believe it to be.

These social meanings I feel are inherent in art and cannot be escaped so long as we are affected by the arts at all. Art can be purgative, curative, educational—or the converse of these. We may be consciously unaware what it is doing to us, but our failure of consciousness cannot close out its effect. The social setting is, then, one larger than the piece of art itself, and it is one in which art may be judged. The criterion is not that it makes us conform to the accepted, for its revelatory reassessment of our acceptances may be its great strength. The criterion we judge it by may not be the world as we have thought it, for again its strength may be in its reappraisal of that world. One criterion, I think, is almost an internal one, the honesty with which its implications are pursued. The other will be its purgative power, its straightening out of our wishes conscious and subconscious, and these will combine, I think, into a very moral generality, whether it make us better men—whatever we choose to mean by that phrase.

CHAPTER 8

The Limits of Analysis

WHAT is in the art and what is in you as you enjoy it, its subject matter, order, and being, and the meanings these induce in you—these the critic must discover. They form the description of the work, and the work must be analyzed to discover them.

One cannot discover anything—except by the purest accident—unless one has an idea what to look for: one finds out by asking questions, and what questions one asks will define what one finds out. Thus all this disquisition so far has tried to show what the nature and some of the capacities of art may be and to suggest therefrom some scheme for asking questions, a way of analysis. A thorough analysis may become a long job for the critic; he will never say all he has found; he cannot even remember all the immediate meanings, what he saw and felt throughout any considerable piece of reading, stage performance, or concert. A poem he can and will reread, so that analysts have often written more about a sonnet than about a novel, having had a chance to re-explore their experience and what caused it; and a picture can be examined at length, of course. Even so, re-examination may shatter one's memory of first experience, may alter primary and strongest effects, may diminish in one's mind the obvious and dominant for later found, more subtle factors in the art and in experience of it.

The problem of analysis is not alone its length but its objectivity. It was because of the excessively personal reactions of critics that what was called the New Criticism sprang up in an attempt to find and talk about what could be objectively substantiated: these words were here and there, those colors and shapes here and there, and so on. At first New Critics tended to distrust their own responses as being of no importance; though they knew they had them, these responses were subjective, not objective. As time has gone on, however, and though not working from response but from the "text," such critics have with extraordinary ingenuity discovered what creates response, until they are effectively speaking of the same things one working from response back to text would speak of. The danger here, I suppose, may come from finding in the text relationships and possible implications which simply do not work out into one's actual response, so that excessive attention has been paid to the textural qualities and more meanings found than the reader or observer could ever react to. Whether this be "objective" becomes a moot question, and whether it results in a just picture of a piece of art may be disputed, too. I am inclined to believe that after the effective training the new critics have given us in what sort of relationships to look for—what questions to ask—a more balanced description may begin by asking what one actually saw and felt and by hunting from these answers into the text for source. Careful analysis, however, may well do very much more than create a description, for by examination of shape and pattern and suggestion it may disclose a writer's skill. Out of this disclosure, since most of us admire skill, may come some feeling of unity and order in one's own sentiments. Furthermore, from such sign of the skillful arrangement of a piece one may get at its various meanings and its major effect. Analysis of the thing rather than of our responses may breed new responses and warmer understanding.

Two other schemes of examination have recently come into literary analysis: the symbolic and the mythical. In a sense Freud started one, and Sir James Frazer the other. For a while every sword, every snake, every cave clearly meant a sexual symbol and so made every story into a story of sex, so that Blake's "Chapel of Gold," as I suggested, was a poem of rape, and the young Arthur pulling the strange sword out of the anvil and sticking it in and pulling it out again was accomplished in some sort of sexual activity. At this point, of course, the mythologist rebelled; he pointed out the antiquity of the magic weapon motif and suggested that its origin came from trials to win the position of the King in early societies, that in bow-using societies the bow was the trial weapon, as in the *Ramayana* and the *Odyssey,* but in sword-using periods it was the sword, as in the *Volsunga Saga.* Perhaps the ability to handle the weapon and to prove one's right to kingship and the duty of impregnating the queen of fertility was a symbolic forecast of sexual prowess, but in the major contest of this kind in the ancient Mesopotamian *Gilgamesh* the combatants use no weapons but wrestle and become friends.

Symbolism of the psychoanalytic kind and of the mythical sort has been the scheme of questions by a good many recent analysts of art. Some of their warrant has come from what seems to be true, that Joyce in his *Ulysses* modeled many of the adventures of his Leopold

Bloom on the adventures of the *Odyssey,* and that since his time, writers like Faulkner and the most devious of Southern writers, Eudora Welty, have used myths, too. To some degree the analysts who hunt for these properties first have seemed to suggest that their presence in a piece of work guarantees value, even the only value. The process of their thought here, I often suspect, goes: "the thing is good; therefore it must have a myth behind it"—which seems to me the wrong sort of thinking. Yet it is true that old mythical situations deriving from man's feeling for his place in nature and from his fear of death do seem to have power as they come out in epics and fairy stories and folk tales. I confess I do not know just what their effectiveness means about the nature of man, and my speculations would be too long to put down here; I can only offer a small skeptic query whether it be not possible to tell a myth badly and whether the order from beginning, through struggle, to decision be not what makes the telling good.

Psychoanalytic investigation, so long as it does not insist that mature men and women act only on the impulses of infancy, may well discover a great many of the reasons things appeal to us. The specifications of the causes of our responses need to be worked out and studied. Yet such investigation is only part of literary analysis, and it does not face up to the critical question whether what immediately appeals to us is what we want or feel we should want; indeed, we may prefer one kind of appeal to another. As I have attempted throughout to suggest, our attitudes and memories, conscious and unconscious, condition what we see and what we feel about what we see.

The critic in his analysis, then, though he may try to hunt for everything in the whole experience of a piece of art, may very often pick out things he especially hunts for. What the piece of art seems to be to one man may be quite different from what it seems to be to another because the questions they each ask are different. The source of those questions will turn out to be, I think, a critical choice of value. One looks for properties in the art that one especially likes or dislikes: "If it's any good, it's got to have this," or "If the good guys win, it's bound to be lousy."

Analysis, then, has trouble remaining objective. Even its investigative questions depend upon an evaluative system. And an evaluative system means a theory of what is good in art. This does not depend on art, for how can you say this piece of art is better than that by their properties alone? Why do you hunt for order or impact or myth as against other qualities? There must be an external cause of predisposition, a set of principles about art, chosen from the diversity of art, perhaps, but by what criterion of choice? I think it will come clear that the choice of criterion depends on what you want art to do to you or for you and that this preference will depend upon what you want art to be in life and what you want life to be.

Let me illustrate the necessity of further considerations with a few examples and brief analyses of them.

The first is a piece from the Scandinavian *Poetic Edda* called "The First Lay of Gudrun," one of the pieces which told moments of the heroic story of the Volsungs and of Sigurd, the Volsung hero. Sigurd had awakened Brynhild from her magic sleep, left her, and gone to the Rhineland; here, after being given a magic potion of forgetfulness, he had married Gudrun. Later Sigurd, still forgetful, had helped Gudrun's brother Gunnar win Brynhild as wife. Brynhild, one day, when she found that the ring she had given Sigurd as a love pledge was on Gudrun's finger, became jealous and in her rage persuaded Gunnar to have Sigurd killed. It is now that Sigurd's wife, Gudrun, laments.

Gudrun of old days
Drew near to dying
As she sat in sorrow
Over Sigurd;
Yet she sighed not
Nor smote hand on hand,
Nor wailed she aught
As other women.

Then went earls to her,
Full of all wisdom,
Fain help to deal
To her dreadful heart:
Hushed was Gudrun
Of wail, or greeting,
But with a heavy woe
Was her heart a-breaking.

Bright and fair
Sat the great earls' brides,
Gold arrayed
Before Gudrun;
Each told the tale
Of her great trouble,
The bitterest bale
She erst abode.

Then spake Giaflaug,
Giuki's sister:
"Lo upon earth
I live most loveless
Who of five mates
Must see the ending,
Of daughters twain

And three sisters
Of brethren eight,
And abide behind lonely."

Naught gat Gudrun
Of wail and greeting,
So heavy was she
For her dead husband,
So dreadful-hearted
For the King laid dead there.

Then spake Herborg
Queen of Hunland—
"Crueller tale
Have I to tell of,
Of my seven sons
Down in the Southlands,
And the eighth man, my mate,
Felled in the death-mead.

"Father and mother,
And four brothers,
On the wide sea
The winds and death played with;
The billows beat
On the bulwark boards.

"Alone must I sing o'er them,
Alone must I array them,
Alone must my hands deal with
Their departing;
And all this was
In one season's wearing,
And none was left
For love or solace.

"Then was I bound
A prey of the battle,
When that same season
Wore to its ending;

As a tiring may
Must I bind the shoon
Of the duke's high dame,
Every day at dawning.

"From her jealous hate
Gat I heavy mocking,
Cruel lashes
She laid upon me,
Never met I
Better master
Or mistress worser
In all the wide world."

Naught gat Gudrun
Of wail or greeting,
So heavy was she
For her dead husband,
So dreadful-hearted
For the King laid dead there.

Then spake Gullrond,
Giuki's daughter—
"O foster-mother,
Wise as thou mayst be,
Naught canst thou better
The young wife's bale."
And she bade uncover
The dead King's corpse.

She swept the sheet
Away from Sigurd,
And turned his cheek
Towards his wife's knees—
"Look on thy loved one
Lay lips to his lips,
E'en as thou were clinging
To thy king alive yet!"

Once looked Gudrun—
One look only,

And saw her lord's locks
Lying all bloody,
The great man's eyes
Glazed and deadly,
And his heart's bulwark
Broken by sword-edge.

Back then sank Gudrun,
Back on the bolster,
Loosed was her head array,
Red did her cheeks grow,
And the rain-drops ran
Down over her knees.

Then wept Gudrun,
Giuki's daughter,
So that the tears flowed
Through the pillow;
As the geese withal
That were in the homefield,
The fair fowls the may owned,
Fell a-screaming.

Then spake Gullrond,
Giuki's daughter—
"Surely knew I
No love like your love
Among all men,
On the mould abiding;
Naught wouldst thou joy in
Without or within doors,
O my sister,
Save beside Sigurd."

Then spake Gudrun,
Giuki's daughter—
"Such was my Sigurd
Among the sons of Giuki,
As is the king leek
O'er the low grass waxing,
Or a bright stone

Strung on band,
Or a pearl of price
On a prince's brow.

"Once was I counted
By the king's warriors
Higher than any
Of Herjan's mays;
Now am I as little
As the leaf may be,
Amid wind-swept wood
Now when dead he lieth.

"I miss from my seat,
I miss from my bed,
My darling of sweet speech.
Wrought the sons of Giuki,
Wrought the sons of Giuki,
This sore sorrow,
Yea, for their sister,
Most sore sorrow.

"So may your lands
Lie waste on all sides,
As ye have broken
Your bounden oaths!

"Ne'er shalt thou, Gunnar,
The gold have joy of,
The dear-bought rings
Shall drag thee to death,
Whereon thou swarest
Oath unto Sigurd.

"Ah, in the days by-gone
Great Mirth in the homefield
When my Sigurd
Set saddle on Grani,
And they went their ways
For the wooing of Brynhild!

An ill day, an ill woman,
And most ill hap!"

Then spake Brynhild,
Budli's daughter–
"May the woman lack
Both love and children,
Who gained greeting
For thee, O Gudrun!
Who gave thee this morning
Many words!"

Then spake Gullrond,
Giuki's daughter–
"Hold peace of such words
Thou hated of all folk!
The bane of brave men
Hast thou been ever,
All waves of ill
Wash over thy mind,
To seven great kings
Hast thou been a sore sorrow,
And the death of good will
To wives and women."

Then spake Brynhild,
Budli's daughter–
"None but Atli
Brought bale upon us,
My very brother
Born of Budli.

"When we saw in the hall
Of the Hunnish people
The gold a-gleaming
On the kingly Giukings;
I have paid for that faring
Oft and full,
And for the sight
That then I saw."

By a pillar she stood
And strained its wood to her;
From the eyes of Brynhild,
Budli's daughter,
Flashed out fire,
And she snorted forth venom,
As the sore wounds she gazed on
Of the dead-slain Sigurd.[1]

This poem depends, of course, in part upon the story. The short verses, accented by the assonant sounds, however, give it a quick and driving quality, especially when it is read aloud and even in translation, here by William Morris. All the pictures are strong and the absoluteness of Gudrun's grief, the diabolic quality of Brynhild come across powerfully, I think. There is no delicacy, there is no subtlety. Oddly enough, there is quite extraordinary order, not at first reading, perhaps, perceptible. After an introductory stanza that places the situation, there is a stanza of action beginning and of Gudrun's attitude. First speaks one woman with a tale of her own losses, a stanza followed by one about Gudrun's reaction. The second example of other women's losses is longer than the first, but Gudrun's reaction is repeated word for word. Then a violent action is done, the baring of Sigurd's corpse, and at the physical center of the poem Gudrun responds to this act: look, revulsion, tears. After a brief speech by a sister about her love, Gudrun turns to speech: of Sigurd, of herself, of the cause of her grief, of prophecy of evil for her evil brothers, and then turns to the major cause of Sigurd's death, Brynhild. Brynhild responds. Gudrun's sister judges Brynhild, and Brynhild lays the curse upon the gold and becomes in picture a sort of venomous dragon figure. This charts into scene and grief; consolation one, failure; consolation two, failure; act, breaking down of Gudrun; speech on cause one; curse on cause one; speech on cause two; curse on cause two; speech by cause two about cause three; return to cause two as evil. The logic of this order, the care with its parts, the compendious treatment of the whole story are, I think, arranged but also powerful.

Out of this order and simplicity and out of the clear images there is an impact on the psyche that is rude and bleak and strong. Only the story, or the derivatives of story, can have such impact, and it is for this impact I have put it here.

The second example is by John Donne, an English poet of the Renaissance, a poem called "Love's Deity."

I long to talk with some old lover's ghost,
Who died before the god of love was born.
I cannot think that he, who then lov'd most,
Sunk so low, as to love one which did scorn.
But since this god produc'd a destiny,
And that vice-nature, custom, lets it be,
I must love her, that loves not me.

Sure, they which made him god, meant not so much,
Nor he in his young godhead practis'd it.
But when an even flame two hearts did touch,
His office was indulgently to fit
Actives to passives. Correspondency
Only his subject was; it cannot be
Love, till I love her, who loves me.

But every modern god will now extend
His vast prerogative as far as Jove.
To rage, to lust, to write to, to commend,
All is the purlieu of the god of love.
O! were we waken'd by this tyranny
To ungod this child again, it could not be
I should love her, who loves not me.

Rebel and atheist too, why murmur I,
As though I felt the worst that love could do?
Love may make me leave loving, or might try
A deeper plague, to make her love me too;
Which, since she loves before, I'm loth to see.
Falsehood is worse than hate; and that must be,
If she whom I love, should love me.[2]

The form of this poem is clearly more designed than that of the first one: stanza form, rhyme, the changes played in the last lines of the stanzas, the very plethora of the word "love," which yet evades monotony. It is a poem without visual sights, only with concepts before the mind. It is, thus, intellectual rather than sensuous. It is in the first person, but it is not so much an expression of personal emotion as of personal mental play. Its ending is a refusal of feeling by its very reversal of the amorous situation. Perhaps it may seem too much a game; perhaps the scarcity of fine language—only a few phrases like "vast prerogative" sound at all "Elizabethan"—may rob it of richness. Yet it is "witty," and for this much admired.

The third example, very short, is another of those Japanese haiku I have used as illustrative:

Flowers by the roadside:
My horse eats them.[3]

The contrast of the human and the animal is obvious. It has, as design, the romantic lifting up of the psyche and the realistic downthrust. Its implications of human aestheticism and animal practicality are so clear as to need no belaboring. It is put here as an example of insight, "truth," knowledge. Since poetry very seldom can offer new knowledge, what it can offer is a new sight, a simple and firm rendition of what one sensed vaguely or had forgotten, or a realization of the "human" importance of relationships of idea. In a simple way this very short poem accomplishes what poetry can do here, I think. And if one wishes to call its comprehension a forerunner of wisdom, one can say that from it one should learn to keep animals out of the flower gardens.

The fourth poem is by C. Day Lewis, an English poet of this century:

Rest from loving and be living.
Fallen is fallen past retrieving
The unique flyer dawn's dove
Arrowing down feathered with fire.

Cease denying, begin knowing.
Comes peace this way here comes renewing
With dower of bird and bud knocks
Loud on winter wall on death's door.

Here's no meaning but of morning.
Naught soon of night but stars remaining
Sink lower, fade, as dark womb
Recedes creation will step clear.[4]

The main effect of this poem is, I think, a call to a future. It was written after the First World War and in a time when it seemed possible to remake the world. What particular future this poem promotes is not easy to guess, but surely the suggestion is forward. This step forward is allied to living, dawn, spring, leaving behind, creation, and ends on the upbeat of "step clear." "Dawn's dove . . . feathered with fire" suggests suddenness, flame burning the old, revelation, a new sacred spirit. Figuratively, emotionally, and in its progression it is a call to change, new birth, new resolution. As such, I take it to be a social poem, a propaganda poem in a way, but for no special program; rather, going from itself into the social world.

The fifth of these examples is a poem in a strict Chinese form by Tu Fu. Let me give it first in a word-for-word translation by Nathan Sivin:

Year end Yin Yang press short light
Heaven edge frost snow clear cold night
Fifth watch drum bugle sound sad lusty
Three gorges stars Milky Way shadows move wave
Wild crying many homes hear fighting attacking
Native songs every where rise fishermen woodcutters
Supine Dragon Leaping Horse end in yellow earth
Human affairs letters books quiet down silent.[5]

I think we can see here the formalism of the poem, which in the original is rhymed in couplets. Even in conventional English the formal qualities still hold:

At the close of the year the forces of nature make the
day short
At the edge of heaven frost and snow clear to a cold night
At the fifth watch the drum and bugle sound sad and lusty
At the Three Gorges the reflections of the Milky Way move
and wave
From many homes comes wild crying at news of fighting,
attacking
Everywhere native songs rise from fishermen and wood-
cutters
Supine Dragon and Leaping Horse have become yellow dust
Human affairs, letters and books, slowly become silent.

The poem is a view from one place; yin and yang are the opposing forces of nature; the Milky Way is what we, too, see, of course, but is also the place to which the

Taoist believes souls go, and therefore suggests the supernatural above and beyond the natural world; the Three Gorges are a well-known scenic spot in China; Leaping Horse and Supine Dragon are nicknames for famous Chinese generals, corresponding to "Old Hickory" for us; the dust to which man returns is yellow or red in Chinese phrase.

The poem is without figure. It relies on simple, realist references, selected by a scheme of natural world, specific sights which reflect "heaven," human acts—war and labor—the famous dead, society which overinvolves us. Its mood is set by the fall into silence of the final line, and that mood, I think, one can call "cosmic," all-inclusive, a large and profound unity. It is, of course, a structural effect, parts becoming suddenly a whole. Such an effect could be achieved with lesser wholes, but where "everything" is put together, I think the word "cosmic" is justified. It is this sort of resolution into a unified satisfactory psychological perspective that some readers find at last most satisfying. One may come out of tragedy and out of a long experience like reading a Dostoevsky novel into a feeling something like this. It is what I noted about the end of Faulkner's "The Bear." It is evident, I think, in a story like Conrad's *The Nigger of the "Narcissus."* Tu Fu's poem is short, of course, and therefore unable to summon up from us the mass of new sights and old recollections that a play or a novel may do, but it becomes, when reread and allowed its time, something like a religious view of things; not Christian, of course, but the Chinese combination of Buddhism and Taoism, recently adumbrated for the Western world in such a novel as Hermann Hesse's *Siddhartha.* I use it here in place of conventional Western philosophic and religious verse as likely to avoid confusing Western readers. Wordsworth among English poets comes closest, perhaps, to this sense of the world.

The final example is a recent poem by X. J. Kennedy, "Nude Descending a Staircase." Such a title was given to a painting by Marcel Duchamp which was the "star" of the famous Armory Show in New York, which introduced "modern art" to America in 1913.

Toe after toe, a snowing flesh,
a gold of lemon, root and rind,
she sifts in sunlight down the stairs
with nothing on. Nor on her mind.

We spy beneath the banister
a constant thresh of thigh on thigh;
her lips imprint the swinging air
that parts to let her parts go by.

One-woman waterfall, she wears
her slow descent like any drape
and pausing on the final stair,
collects her motions into shape.[6]

This poem begins with motion, keeps suggesting it with words like sifts, thresh, swinging, parts go by, waterfall, descent; it neatly and almost mechanically "collects her motions" into the stopping point of "shape." What is given to the reader is visual sights, and the tone is kept objective, perhaps just a little humorous, for "nor on her mind" both repudiates any emotional or dramatic importance to her motion and is a small joke *at* her. For the life of me I can find no external significance in it; all my attempts to ascribe outer meaning fail. Yet it is attractive and memorable, not only in phrases like "parts to let her parts go by" but in its whole picture. I put it here because it seems to me quite "abstract," quite a piece of art for art's sake, unassuming and unprotesting and not at all "exotic," as so much of "art for art's sake" stuff used to be.

The effects of such poems may be matched with those of pictures, and, I suppose, with those of pieces of music. The lament of Gudrun, for instance, in its strength delivers the kind of blow which Goya's picture called "Cronos" does (Figure 12). There is a story behind the picture, of course, the story of the old god devouring his sons because a prophecy had foretold his supplanting by one of them, and a knowledge of the story sets and justifies the picture. Yet it would be strong even by itself, for the

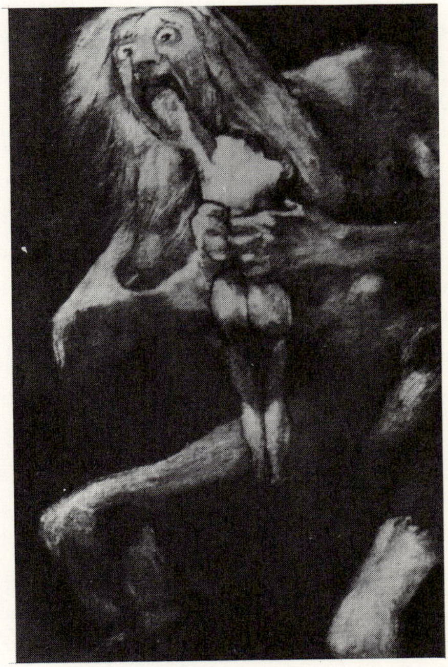

FIGURE 12. "Cronos" by Francisco Goya y Lucientes, Prado Museum, Madrid

design of uprights and cross motions, the central illumination of the staring-eyed god and the small white body of his son, and the exaggerations of body and face are enough to strike attention. Certain sorts of critic will regard it as melodrama, of course, too excessive a play for emotion, and it is out of the mainstream of European painting; yet its power, like the power of William Blake, may be exciting even to those who finally turn against it.

"Serious" painting has seldom been witty. The cartoonist has seemed to pre-empt the place of wit, and the cartoonist has been regarded as a man with a political ax to grind. I find myself, however, regarding Picasso as a wit very often, his reassortments of human anatomy seeming to me more intellectual play than sober commentary and than startling design. True, he likes to shock as well as amuse, but this picture in blue and sand tones of what may be mother and daughter at the seashore, with the paternal face looming over the water's horizon, I take to be more wit than design, though strong in that, and the playing with bulbosities and angularities an amusing game (Figure 13). (The picture may also be taken as two females slyly establishing their innocence with a child's toy boat and the masculine prey wary but interested—a study in the games of the seaside.)

For the correspondence to the haiku let me use a somewhat more substantial piece of visual art, by which I hope I can more clearly and more shortly establish the kind of comprehension art is especially apt to give. This is the bust of Niccolo da Uzzano long thought to be by the Florentine sculptor Donatello (Figure 14). A bust is by necessity a simple design, head, neck, shoulders. Here the head is turned a little to the left and thrust a little forward, with the shoulders themselves held a little high and back. No gesture is excessive, but each diverges

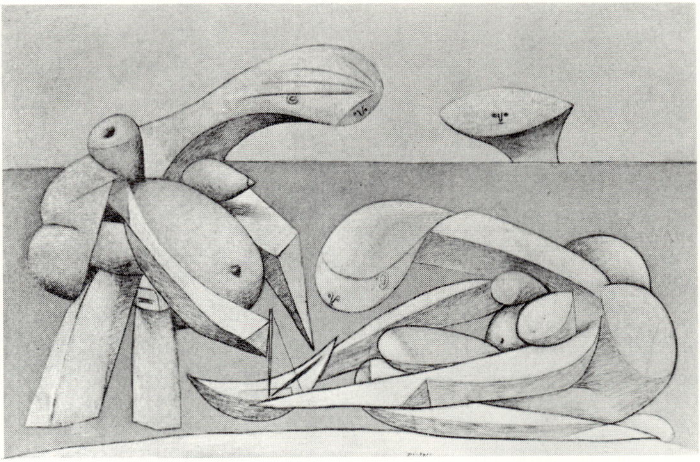

FIGURE 13. "Bathers" by Pablo Picasso, Peggy Guggenheim Collection, Venice. Courtesy of Miss Guggenheim

from the normal enough to suggest vitality. The head is bony, yet it is not fleshless and gaunt. The face is long; the eye sockets, the nose, the upper lip, the jaw are all a little more than normally large; the forehead, hence, becomes a little low, the Mediterranean as against the Teutonic type, yet whatever is suggested by the short forehead is counterbalanced by the large eye sockets and the low setting of the eyes. The mouth is straight across, the lower lip fuller than the upper; the low ears tend to offset the triangularity of the head and spread out the whole. The neck is actually rather large, but the lowering of the clavicle and the accentuation of the tendon up from it break the sense of size, and the slight straightening of that tendon toward the jaw maintains a sense of strength. The bust is painted in subdued colors, without the shine of stone or the harshness of bronze.

The bust has a series of forward thrusts and pulls backward. The head, held up and forward, is neither active

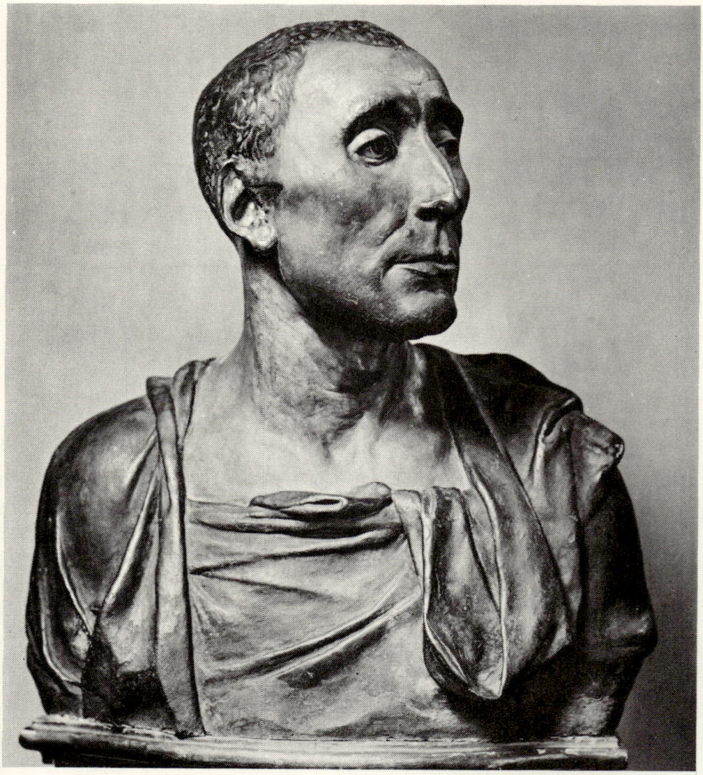

FIGURE 14. "Niccolo da Uzzano" by Donatello, The Bargello, Florence. Photograph by permission of Fratelli Alinari

nor arrogant. The eyes are cold, perhaps, yet interested, the mouth decisive yet warm enough in the lower lip and with just a hint of humor in the right corner (the left as viewed). The man of the bust could be cruel and rapacious, yet intelligent and just and productive. Niccolo himself was a condottiere, or hired military man, but also a respected political worker for Florence. The bust suggests to me that kind of person society seems incapable of doing without, on one side decisive and ruthless, on the other constructive, the type of the first Rockefeller, perhaps. As I look at the six-inch copy of the original two-foot bust which I have long had on the mantelpieces of the homes I have lived in, I think I am made to comprehend this kind of character (Figure 15). (Perhaps comprehension is always the reconciliation of dichotomies.)

One could say of Donatello's bust that he had a good model to work from, but I think Donatello could reply, "But see what I made of him!" Within the seeming representation of the bust slight shifts and organizations, which balance directions of character, make implications and bring comprehension. Perhaps no short poem can do so much, but the Japanese haiku enters this class of art. Both are more "thoughtful" than they seem at first.

Visual art has often been deliberately used for social

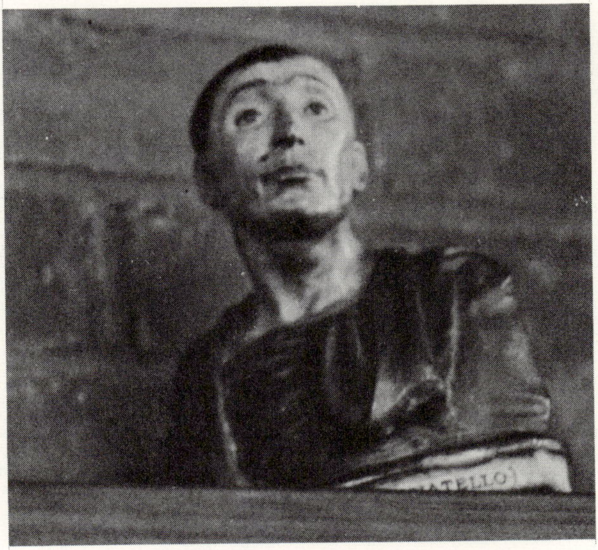

FIGURE 15. Plaster copy of Donatello's bust

effects. These range from the social idealism implicit in much ancient Greek sculpture to the obvious hortatory nature of Communist "realism," and end in advertising art. C. Day Lewis' poem is not so clearly social as pictures of the downtrodden or pictures of the gay, healthy, and young which encourage soft drinks and trips to sunny islands. José Clemente Orozco's murals in the Baker Library at Dartmouth College are more violent and more committed to a program, perhaps, than Lewis' poem (Figure 16). The series of pictures treats the his-

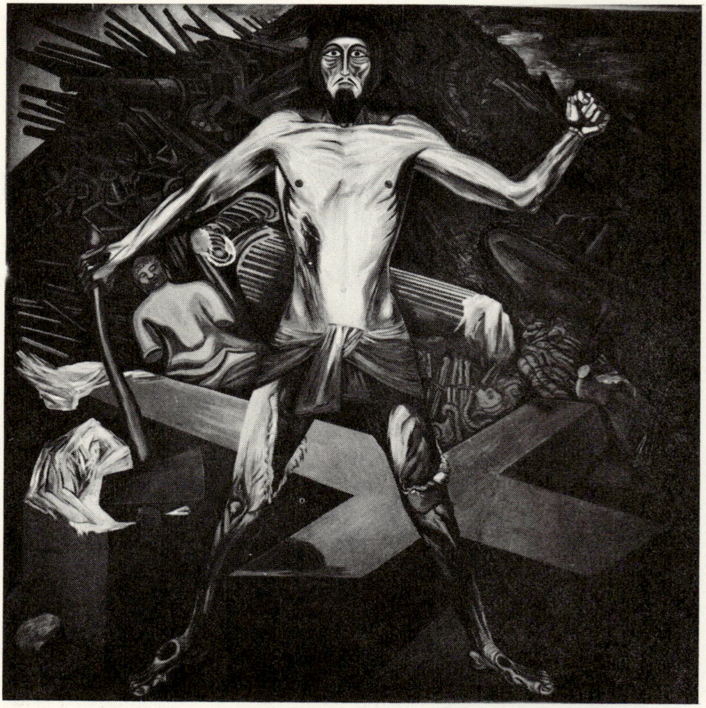

FIGURE 16. From the mural "Modern Migration of the Spirit" by José Clemente Orozco, Baker Library, Dartmouth College, Hanover, N.H. Courtesy of the Trustees of Dartmouth College

tory of the Mexicans: arrival, the white god, Cortez, United States domination by money and soldiers, exhausted education, and the First World War, ending in this Christ who has destroyed all the old civilizations, even his own cross. This summary panel, this angry, rerisen, and ominously colored Christ with the Byzantine solemnity of face and the angularity of his destructive ax against the broken world behind him is a general repudiation of long injustice and inhumanity. It may not have the lift of heart of Lewis' poem, for all its sights are harsh, yet repudiation of the past implies, I think, a resolution for the future. The picture is more of a blow to one's response than the poem, but the two are in somewhat the same area of art and both may be admired for their social importance.

In companionship with Tu Fu's poem one could put many Chinese landscapes, with their attention to hills, trees, and water, their half-hidden little buildings, tiny boats and fishermen, and small contemplative philosophers. These are visual brothers of the poem. Yet let me put here again, perhaps only because I am very fond of it, a Maitreya, or Compassionate Buddha of the Future, from the Boston Museum of Fine Arts (Figure 17). The statue is formal, very thin front to back, its folded legs hardly distinguishable as such, its ornaments arranged symmetrically, its head very large for its body, and its remaining hand likewise. The face is very simply and sharply carved, held a little forward and eyes outlooking. It is not an amused face, nor a commanding face, nor one that tries to dominate. It is a face that seems to bring one back from excess to "perspective." It is almost as patterned as the face of Orozco's Christ, but against the Orozco open eye and the Orozco set mouth and lined cheeks it sets the half-open eye, the full-lipped mouth,

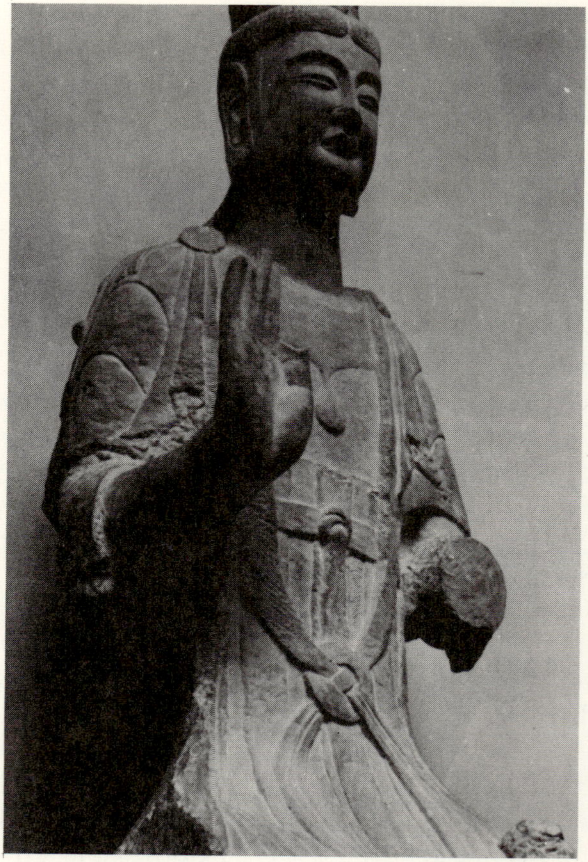

FIGURE 17. The Buddha "Maitreya" (See Figure 2, page 9). Courtesy of the Museum of Fine Arts, Boston

half firm, half kindly, and the full, restful cheeks. It is a formal statue, certainly, but the formality gives way after a time to an embracing humanity and control and sense both of assurance and of unity. It has a more religious tone than Tu Fu's poem, perhaps, and the natural setting takes no place directly here, but the two, poem and statue, share a gift of integration of all things, I think.

Beside Mr. Kennedy's poem of the nude descending the stairs one could put much of the art of recent times. Let me put, however, one of the several paintings of "Nude Descending a Staircase" which Marcel Duchamp did and which, of course, inspired Mr. Kennedy's poem (Figure 18). The human form is broken up into planes and tubes which are arranged in a sort of funnel shape down and to the right to give a sense of motion. One can feel this motion, if only now and then, perhaps. I find no external meaning in the picture, any more than in the poem, but a tone a good deal less humanly interested, a tone of analysis forecasting the reassortments that have fascinated Picasso for so many years, a tone, however, less amused or angry than Picasso was to display, and indeed less interested in the aesthetics of arrangement than in the analysis of the body in motion under light.

The end of this sort of pictorial dehumanization seems to me to have been the stark and simple geometry of Mondrian (Figure 19), where from a painting like this one the only human voice is one that repudiates all feeling and replaces it with the impersonal purity of mathematics. No poem can quite do this, I think; surely Mr. Kennedy's does not try, for unless one keeps beside his poem very clearly the Duchamp picture, one feels his nude as a woman after all. Yet Mr. Kennedy is not trying to say anything *about* the woman or about life from the woman. In a sense the Mondrian picture protests "how pure and incorrupt I am!" Kennedy does not do that to me, nor does he encapsulate "life." Duchamp is clearly analyzing human forms in a "scientific" way. Kennedy is not even doing that. Mondrian's formal arrangement is very simple, very logical but very simple, not boring because asymmetrical and subtly balanced. I find Kennedy's poem more complex and equally ordered. Both of

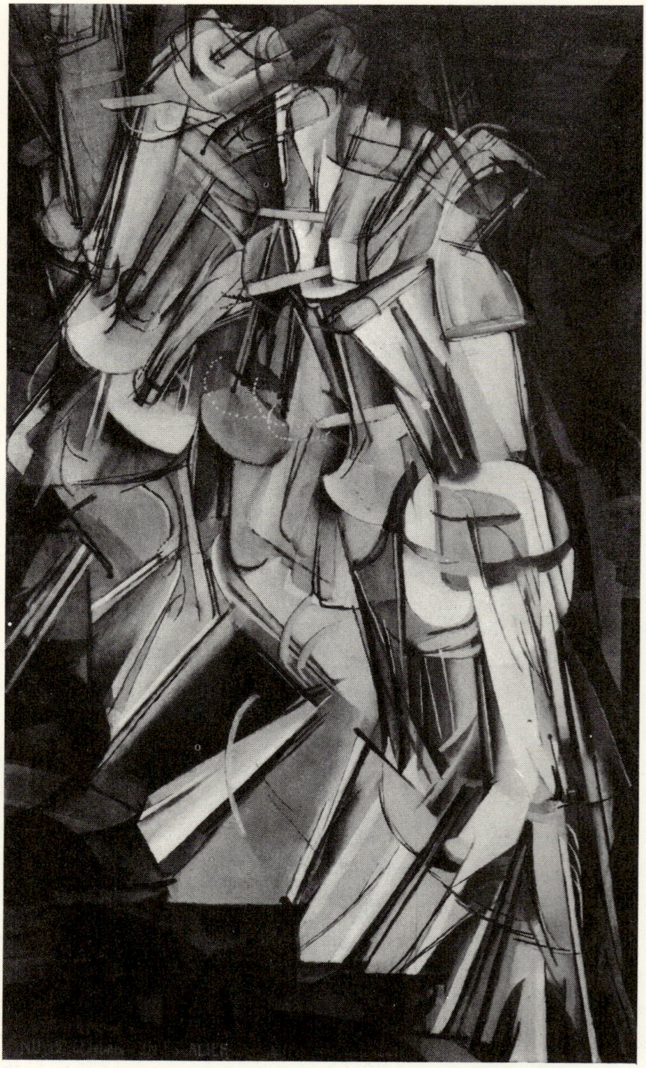

FIGURE 18. "Nude Descending a Staircase, No. 2" by Marcel Duchamp. Louise and Walter Arensberg Collection, Philadelphia Museum of Art. Courtesy of the Philadelphia Museum of Art

these seem to me "purer" as art than Duchamp's use of a picture for analytic purposes.

Here, then, are six kinds of art, each with its own major effect and each effect agreeing with its own view of what art should be. One could extend the list and subdivide the kinds of appeal, but perhaps these will serve to illustrate the problem of choice. None of these seems to me negligible in form, negligible in technique, negligible in the experience it gives, or not a piece of art in its own

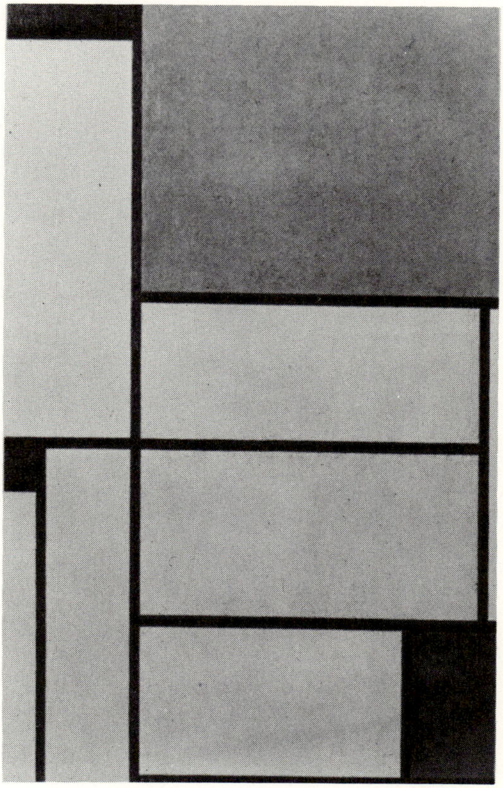

FIGURE 19. "Tableau One" by Piet Mondrian, in private collection, Basel

right, whether one wishes to give it external meaning or not. One can say C. Day Lewis' poem goes out beyond itself, but it also gives a kind of "lift to the heart" that has no external conclusion except as it does lift the heart. I have, of course, used it here as a poem that can be taken as promoting a position, as quite clearly Orozco's picture does. The others seem to me as self-sufficient as art is likely on the average to be.

It is easy enough to say they are all fine poems and fine pictures and let them go with that acclaim. Yet few will like them all equally. Most of us will have preferences. Is it possible to give any objective judgment on them? Is there a universal criterion?

I can hear voices saying about Gudrun's lament that it is impressive but what does it mean?, and a voice in answer asking, "Doesn't its moving of the psyche about bereavement, about evil, make it 'profound'? What can one ask more than experience, more than being made to feel the power of human grief?"

This second voice will light on John Donne's poem and complain that its wit is easy, its cynicism shallow; and a third voice will say, "Ah, but how balanced a view of the world after all! How neatly it punctures romantic pretensions and silly fashions! and, unexpressed, what an ideal of love!"

Perhaps this voice will say of the haiku that it's just a cute joke after all, and in answer, he who likes this sort of comprehension will admire the breadth of view the few words and the simple scene engender.

Mr. Lewis' poem will be defended both by those who feel art must be a part of society and those who want a good and hopeful feeling about things. Both will be scorned by the contemplative man who regards excess protestation and momentary stimulus of the mind as unbalanced and perhaps, even, a little gauche. This man will find the broad but passive mood of Tu Fu's poem the most attractive.

And finally, the "true artist" will scorn the appeals to emotion and to idea of all the pieces but the last set, whose "literary," "poetic," "artistic," "musical" quality, whose essential "thing-ness" will seem to him more worthy than the possibly vulgar effects of the others.

How can one adjudicate here? It is a question of each man to his taste, each man to his own choice. Yet, perhaps, there is some reason besides caprice for taste, if not in everyone, then in the more mature and consistent personalities.

It is such reason that I must now try to explore.

CHAPTER 9

The Philosophical Bases of Choice

PERHAPS the way to get at this whole subject of the basis of criticism is to begin with what several sorts of people will ask art to do for them. All men may agree that art is in some way "fun," a pleasure, but men's definitions of pleasure run from the violently sensual to the complicated and cerebral. I suppose, indeed, that any conscious fabrication can give someone "fun," its maker if no one else. Pleasure is a very shifty criterion, but we must explore what we can of it.

Let me narrowly define pleasure here as some effect on the nerves that has no necessary implication beyond that effect: that is, pleasure is the activity of the psyche uncomplicated by side effects or aftereffects. As such we might call it sensation. All of us distinguish sensations we like from those we don't like, and perhaps we could generalize a good way here: few of us would like the sensation of being stung by a bee or of watching a friend die. Such sensations we call pain. Yet we are so various that only the extremes of good and bad will be accepted or rejected by any great majority. And art is something other than life in a way that makes it possible for us to be "pleasantly" stirred by the stage death of a man we are more or less in favor of.

Those who feel that art should give them "pleasure," however they define it, want, quite simply, to "feel good." They wish to be "involved," to be "touched." Some of them are so catholic in their tastes that they are very nearly willing to cross out "good" after "feel"; any experience that results in that distinctive narrowing and centralizing of the psyche we call "feeling" will be a "good" experience. Such seekers after experience I find to be, in art, rather the makers than the critics. I don't know that I could enlarge this to say creators in any area of human activity are likely to be ones with very little discrimination among sensations, for I have short evidence to go on, but I think it likely that an artistic creator will be, first off, a seeker of experience per se, perhaps because the critical discrimination that will cringe from the unpleasant will prevent the explorations and the comprehensions that the artist may need.

Most people are not creators of art, however; most people like "good" sensations. There will be, as I have suggested, great diversity among canons of "good," and one man may look with wonder at the bridge-player or chess-player who exerts with delight the whole of his psyche in what this first man would call "work," and I myself look with equal wonder at a young acquaintance who likes to run marathons. Yet all four of us might ask of art that it give us pleasure. We would be joined, I am sure, by a great many who would say about a piece of art, "Yes, it's bright and orderly and significant and all that, but it doesn't make me feel a thing." Indeed, I suspect that this criterion of feeling or "good" feeling is by all odds the major criterion among all who look at art. The various statements of poets and writers of all sorts that they know a thing is "good" as art if it makes the hair rise up at the neck or goose pimples rise on the flesh show how widespread even among artists is this test of really rather simple sensation.

Yet the simplicity of the effect must not be taken to imply the simplicity of the causes of it. The hair of the poet, I take it, would not rise at obvious or banal causes; the "hair-raising" thing would not be the violent or the sentimental or the simply organized. Thus it might take the unusual, the lengthy, the complex to force the psyche to pour its energy into that central fixity which would raise the hair. I know a lady whose "hackles" rise most strongly at two lines from Blake's "The Tiger":

When the stars threw down their spears,
And watered heaven with their tears.[1]

Very often, I suspect, such sensations arise inexplicably: one knows "a bell rings," but why it rings one cannot tell.

There is no one factor in art that produces feelings or "good" feelings. The immediate meanings may do it, the sights and sounds and attitudes that come first to mind. As the colors in an abstract painting may overwhelm us, so the sound patterns of poetry may halt our attention and move us: one can chant "Let me not to the marriage of true minds" and half sing "go and catch a falling star" without an "idea" in one's head but with a feeling of pleasure: so the shapes of a tree in a Chinese picture or the feel of a snowy road in Hemingway or, a longer example, the sights of the great strike scene in Zola's *Germinal*. In a more complicated and less visual way the long, modified, oral sentences of Faulkner that one works out best reading aloud may be a pure delight as one reconstructs and "grasps" them. For some critics these textural effects are all-important.

I suppose, however, that the most common cause of good sensations comes from the operation of the psychic curve of design, particularly toward its crisis, when one becomes aware of the connotations of alternative action, when one becomes aware of what is "riding" on the crisis both for the actors in the story and for the reader. For me, I think, the most powerful of feelings comes from that sort of conclusion which brings the world together, what I have called a "cosmic" unity in speaking of the last part of Faulkner's "The Bear," or when the cosmos of Shakespeare's Cleopatra comes to its end in Iras' ". . . the bright day is done and we are for the dark," or when, by some means I cannot fully tease out, Homer's *Iliad* comes to a focus on the final words: "Such was the funeral of Hector, tamer of horses."

I suggest, then, that in literature events are the commonest cause of feeling. Aristotle was probably right in thinking "action" the dominant factor. Yet the more or less sudden rise in heartbeat we call warmth, the outward mark of inner feeling, may be brought on by pieces of action, by comprehensions of situation, by just "the way the words go." Whatever the cause, that the feeling appear—pleasant, good, hair-raising, tear-bringing—will be the final and overriding demand many people will make of art, and that it do this will be their idea of art's place.

Even those who demand sensations of pleasure, however, may not regard those sensations as the *sine qua non.* I have an invaluable rule about books and movies and plays: if they make me cry—and I love to cry happy tears, even sorrowful ones, at art—I know they're not really first class. I know that in a few hours perhaps a warm memory will last, but I will feel a little let down, a little fooled. I am sure that many, with better discrimination than mine, with more mature personalities, will not really cry at all. The threshold of their gift of self to the art will be higher than mine. Yet what we all demand here may be a sense of "significance." This is not a very clear word. I suppose it means that we find connotations, make relations from this thing before us to other things in the world. "Signify," "import," "connote,"—"typify," even—have a family of meanings. So I suggested, far back in this treatise now, that "Yesterday the first daffodil bloomed" brought things to mind as "yesterday I scratched my ear" did not. So I found meaning or import in

In the mountain village
Under the piled-up snow
The sound of water.

whereas I am pretty sure that I wouldn't find much in

In the crowded streetcar
Over the chatter of wheels
A no-smoking sign.

What seems significant or important may be the reference of what is before us outward to the kind of thing I have called an external meaning; we go from this to that other or to those others. We generalize out. The process, however, may be from out inward; the art may call up to mind a number of things—"important" things about which we may have many or central feelings and attitudes—and may then use these connotations as the matter the piece organizes and completes. So, I suppose, the *Iliad* takes the various feelings aroused in us by Hector as leader and father and husband and son and brother and defender of Helen and man of courage and man of impetuosity and man of occasional cowardice, his victories and his runnings away and his death, and the lamentations of Hecuba and Helen and brings them somehow all together on the unifying last line of the poem. I think I do not go out *from* the *Iliad;* I have been out and around and come back to the completed events as themselves. So, though here more hesitantly, I believe that at the end of my journey outward from

Old pond:
Frog-jump-in
Water-sound.

I return at last inward just to the scene again. Either way, as outward or inner meaning, the feelings we have about men in their closest sorts of relations and the feelings we have about the vast physical world and the fragile animate one inside it give significance to the *Iliad* and to Basho's little poem. Perhaps it is here unnecessary to distinguish very much the internal use from the external reference—though I think that, either way, something decisive and consummatory must be done about these connotations to make them seem significant. The point here is the reason why we want the significant. In part, I suppose, it is that the significant, in signifying more, stimulates more of the brain's memories and so, in some way no one seems to understand, floods more energy into the center the work has been organized for. The pleasure-lover will say he gets more of a "bang" from an important thing than from an unimportant one: it's not always easy to get excited about the election of a town meeting member, but one can hardly refrain from some excitement about the election of a national president.

In another part I suppose we want the significant because we want to be "educated." One may not be consciously aware of this sort of motive; one may refrain from saying or thinking that one learns from the piece of art. We are, many of us, however, in some uncertainty about many of the concerns of human life—who is good or bad, what to do, how to feel, what to think, and so on—and we may feel that the unimportant has hardly been "worth our while"—even though it has made us laugh or cry or suffer or be roused. It is so that many of us feel about the "average" movie; though we were not bored, though we were even excited and were happy over the outcome, we may have felt we were wasting an evening. So, many people look with some scorn at the detective story, the "pastime of great minds." The important gives us something to think about, chew over, absorb into our view of the world: learn from. We may treat it as a sort of hypothesis, a "maybe," a potentiality, and begin trying it out on life and seeing how things look from its point of view.

An art critic named Clive Bell a couple of generations ago used the words "significant form"; T. S. Eliot somewhat later talked of "significant emotion." I fancy both were talking roughly about the same thing, the kind of effect the internal texture and pattern and order of a piece might arouse without external reference. The linear symbols for a splash of water done by a newspaper cartoonist, two or three swift curving lines and a few unpatterned blob shapes, and the linear symbols done by a Japanese artist, lines a little irregular, varied in width, straightening and almost rectangular, with graded and patterned broken drops, will differ in care of execution but also in the sense of vigor they rouse: more will happen over a longer time when looking at the Japanese drawing than at the cartoonist's; hence the Japanese drawing will be more "significant" in feeling from its form (Figure 20). Significant, then, need not stand for

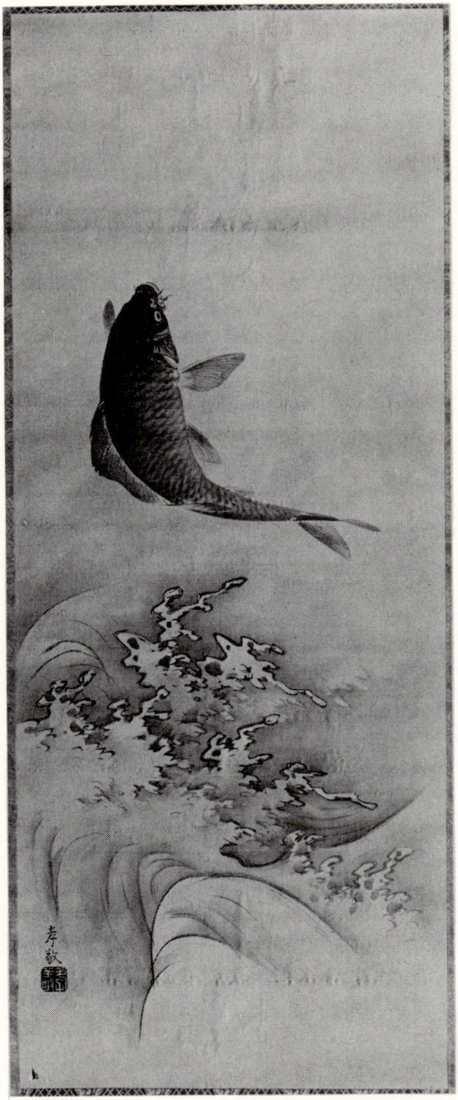

FIGURE 20. "Carp Leaping," Japanese painting by Kokei. Courtesy of the Museum of Fine Arts, Boston

a connotation of important human issues but only an idea-less and extensive psychic response. The Japanese drawing may say no more about water, but it will say indirectly something about variety and vigor and order in us and in the world. We can learn, do learn from such effects on us. We may only be aware that one gives us more and pleasanter sensations than the other.

Significant, then, implies some sort of enlargement of our experience, whether as idea or feeling or perception. To want such enlargement seems to me to want some form of education or "improvement." When we speak of education, we are inclined to think of knowledge, ideas, concepts. When we speak of improvement, we may be inclined to think of attitudes, feelings, adjustments for action. It is very easy to stick "moral" in as an adjective in front of improvement, and morality seems to have something less to do with knowledge than with feeling or the remembrances of feeling we call attitude, but improvement may be essentially cognitive.

Art is not much given to the dispensing of knowledge. Indeed, I suppose one distinction between literary art and the discourse of the essay is the absence in one and presence in the other of overt knowledge. Knowledge implies some sort of intellectual ordering of its information; many things of one sort are brought together and related to make knowledge. Knowledge remains, however, largely impersonal and somewhat static; anyone may achieve the knowledge another man has, for it is objective, about something outside of one. Even when a man says he has knowledge of himself or of his past, he sees himself as an object outside himself, as one can look quite objectively at one's toe and feel it is as distinct from oneself as a chair leg. Knowledge is concerned with something external to oneself, to one's interests, and for itself. If one examines his feelings when, in some novels, a character gives a sort of lecture, one will discover, I think, a cessation of those attitudes and tensions with which one has been following the actions and situations of the characters and a concentration now outside the novel on what the character is lecturing about. The presentation of knowledge can be said to interfere with art.

Knowledge, then, cannot be a demand we make of art. Though we may say we learn about men from Shakespeare, we do so not directly but by another process than simple communication, for Shakespeare was not writing treatises but plays. What we get from art is something we call "comprehension" or "understanding." For this not very much detail may be needed, nothing like the number of pieces of information that knowledge requires. What one has of this, however, is not simply related to itself, internally related, as in knowledge—you can know a lot about butterflies without knowing much about anything else—but externally related to the "rest of the world" and especially to oneself. Comprehension does not focus on the thing alone but on the thing in relation to other things and to oneself. One only "understands" butterflies in relation to the rest of the world. Comprehension occurs finally in a unitary flash; it is globular and in itself a sort of work of art. I think that once attained it is less separable into parts than knowledge is and seems thus more like feeling than like concept. It is often unverbalizable, hence incommunicable. A writer can give you his knowledge; a writer cannot quite give you his comprehension; he can, however, make you comprehend, can suggest ways for you to create your own comprehension. So Conrad in the famous preface to *The Nigger of the "Narcissus"* said he wanted ". . . above all to make you *see*," a verb for a state immediate, personal, clear, and wordless. "See," "understand," "comprehend"—these are words for what the artist can hope to make us do and for what we can demand of art.

The artist, of course, generally deals with particulars, particular characters and events, particularly aroused feelings, or generalities so treated as to seem particulars. I suppose it possible to do otherwise, but the record has favored the particular. Even when a poet writes

Brightness falls from the air
Queens have died young and fair
Dust hath closed Helen's eye

he focuses on his own feeling by

I am sick. I must die

before his tag line

Lord have mercy on us.[2]

And when a poet wishes to express the general truth that nature is destructive, he speaks to one flower:

O rose, thou art sick!
The invisible worm
That flies in the night
In the howling storm. . . .[3]

The comprehension one creates for oneself from the particulars of literature is, first of all, a comprehension of *this* character, *this* situation, *this* succession of events. We "understand" Macbeth, knowing very little detail about him. As I have heretofore suggested, it is not until later, faced with another particular, that we generalize and say Shakespeare has made us "understand men." Yet, even in the seeing of the play, we may experience a coming together into a globe of sight we call comprehension, not of all men or other men as yet but of Macbeth in relation to his world and to us. Some men will put this in the class of knowledge; some will put it in the class of internal structure, an order like the unity of a picture or a bowl.

Ideal comprehension would be universal, a seizing together of all, I suppose. For this, or for some approximation of this, we would use the word wisdom. Wisdom also implies, I think, a dynamic quality: one understands things and also likelihoods; one acts or decides out of wisdom. Wisdom is, then, inherently moral, if, as I do, one defines morality as knowing what one wants and how to reach it.

Comprehension one can ask of art. It may be too much to ask wisdom of it. We use the word about books occasionally; more often we use it, I think, about the man behind the book: we go through the book to the author. This implies that wisdom inheres somewhere in the author's tone, the way he sees the actions of his characters, the way he sees the succession of his events. We would be less likely to use the word wisdom about a single poem or about a short story; neither would have time to make us see many relationships, and the flat statement of great truths—we, too, will die quickly like the daffodils—may seem more obvious than wise. We may use the word occasionally about unusual combinations of ideas in one poem, yet the attribution of wise is likely to be given to a poet's work as a whole. Indeed, it forms the main argument of much criticism of a writer when he is old or has died; looking back over a lifetime of work, the critic tends to neglect the artistry of his subject for what the man thought about things and how valid that was. In a recent compilation of criticism of Robert Frost, most of it written after Frost's major work had been done, it seemed to me that the chief interest of the critics, even when they were concerned with his phraseology or his poetic structure, was the implication from word and shape and tone about Frost's view of life and its validity.

It is seldom, I think, that one speaks of a wise picture or a wise painter. Yet one could use the term about Rembrandt, not only because his light and shade bring his people out into a remarkable vitality, or because he refuses the heroic for the human, but because, even in his landscape sketches and etchings, he denies that life is full of romantic heights and awful chasms, because his peculiar balance and control and unassuming quality say things about life that sound like wisdom. And I suspect what I was trying to show about Donatello's "Niccolo da Uzzano" was a quality of mind close to wisdom, a way of making me see Niccolo that said, if I verbalize it out from unverbal attitudes: "Don't underestimate or overestimate him; recognize his value in society as well as his threat." I suspect something of the sort could be worked out from music. We use words like "thoughtful" and "contemplative" about pieces of music—among many other adjectives expressive of states of mind—and it would not be hard to show that what lies behind our language is a feeling that the composers saw life in a way we might use the word wisdom for.

That art of all sorts can be made by our interpretive powers to enter that area of the mind we can put somewhere under the label of the cognitive seems to me pretty clear. Thus an intellectual stress, mixed up through our emotional responses, of course, can be asked of art. Indeed, this sort of stress, that it say something about life and men in life, however indirectly, or that it make us say something to ourselves about life—as Basho's little poem makes me say to myself—or that it use what it draws from us of our ideas of life for its own structural purposes is likely to be, in the long run, the major criterion for many who look at art.

Beyond the sensations of pleasure and beyond the cognitive of comprehension there seems to me one other sort of demand men have long made of the arts, especially of the literary ones. This is not unrelated to the cognitive, not unrelated to wisdom in a way, but the stress is rather less upon seeing than upon feeling; it loses some of the remaining objectivity of comprehension for a subjective straightening out. It is, in a way, less concerned with what is than what should be. This is the moral demand, but I have suggested wisdom is ultimately moral, so that I must change my words here a little and call this stress therapeutic. There is a suggestion of improvement in it; those who ask this see therapy as a way of life.

I have previously suggested the purgative power of tragedy and of comedy, that in some way these reorganize and straighten out our psyches by their acting out our evil wishes and our foolish attitudes. I have tried to suggest, too, that what we accept or refuse to accept in our feelings when set against our sense of the world, our judgment of sentimental or not so, may change our attitudes, make us reassess our feelings, may give us new sympathies, understandings, discriminations. Such effects are inescapable, though we may be unaware of them. So, too, the "ideal" may transform us: this statue of a young man, this story of action may show us a way of aspiration, a kind of person to be, a way to act. Though not purgative by showing us the falsity of the mistaken, they are the positive that may pull us in another way. Indeed, a purgative comedian like Molière often put in his plays a reasonable character—often a maid of the house—who represented the proper or ideal way to act. Though the recent temper has been to scorn the "model" man as a sort of insipid propaganda figure, the very scorners by implication set up their own ideal. The purgative by eradicating the negative, and the idealizing by emphasizing the positive, are performing like functions in the improvement of men.

By a twist of view one can, I think, suggest that all art in some degree can be seen as showing a way to go or not to go. And criticism itself is a making conscious and judging the value of these implications. An abstract painting suggests that to see things without the emotional involvements of humanity, without feelings about good or bad, is a proper way to see things. If one would have doubts about living one's life in a room surrounded by a large-scale computer, what would one think of living surrounded by the "abstract," the externally meaningless shapes and colors of nonrepresentational painting, of listening to the inhuman and unrhythmic sounds of computer-made music, or of seeing plays with masked dehumanized characters? Any piece of art can, then, be seen by those who wish to see it so as a moral commentary and may be judged by one's sense of the validity of that effect.

Thus one can ask, not comprehension of what is, so much as direction, leadership, improvement. There are fools, and we wish to be cleansed of our folly; there are evil wishes, and we wish to be purged of them; there are false views of the world, and we wish to be straightened out; there are ways not to go and ways to go, and we wish to follow the proper way. It is easy to say art has nothing to do with such forms of therapy, but perhaps they exist in art, and perhaps many people will consciously seek them.

The sensational, the cognitive, the therapeutic emphases of art seem to me the major final choices one must select from, the final demands, after the demands for experience and order and selfhood, that one can make of art.

What sorts of people will choose which? Here we enter the confusing area of men's choices of purpose, choices dependent on views of the nature of the world and of men, the area of philosophy. This disquisition, of course, is no place to categorize philosophic viewpoints in any accurate and authoritative way, yet one must suggest the various bents or tendencies of mind that are likely to characterize men.

The first of these, and by all odds the largest, I would suggest, is the bent which regards the purpose of life as pleasure, the hedonist. Hedonists may not find life to *be* pleasure; they may suffer and be disappointed and bitter; but they will feel that life ought to be fun of some sort, that happiness—the goal of Aristotle, for instance—is the end of man, the pursuit of it an "inalienable" right. They may regard art as an escape from their vale of tears, as a respite, like their cocktails after the sweat of the day. Such men will want from art, the chances are, that sense of feeling good which sights and sounds and a satisfactory psychic curve can give. Some of them like their whiskey straight, so to speak, like to be hit hard, and will prefer of those things heretofore discussed the sharp strokes to their psyches. They will want intensity rather than diversity. Others of the pleasure-seeking kind may be more gentle in their tastes, may refuse the sharpness of the old Norse sorrow and prefer to loiter in their sipping of the gentler effects of Tu Fu's poem, an effect of unity, cosmic, perhaps contemplative, never vulgar. Another sort of hedonist, one who regards himself as rather hard to touch, would like the wit of the Donne piece, for his delight professes to be in the balance, cleanness, suggestiveness of the art. But then, each of the other pieces will be admired by one or another for its pleasure, for a variety of hedonists will have a variety of pleasures.

There is, of course, a pleasure in comprehension, in meeting, surrounding, organizing, "conquering" the new and perhaps disorderly. There is a pleasure in the exercise and resolution of the psyche, not likely to raise the hair on the back of one's neck but of some less sudden sort; there is a rather complacent pleasure in thinking one understands, a remnant from our egocentric and aggressive youth when we began to realize our separateness and its connotations. Yet I think it only just to grant that the sense of pleasure from either cause may be only a minor part of what occupies the psyche in comprehension, that comprehension itself may be the desideratum. Here, then, we must be aware of a line that can be crossed: is it the feeling good because we comprehend, or is it the comprehension itself that we want? Is it the sense of pleasure at a unified view of the world we get from Tu Fu's poem that we want or the view of the world as view of the world? Is it an internal or an external meaning? Plato's contention that the thing man would least wish to sacrifice was his right to know has been accepted by many men who regard understanding, the awareness of understanding, perhaps, as the supreme good in life. The goal of man is not happiness but awareness, knowing, a development of consciousness, not toward virtue except as virtue is linked to knowledge, but simply toward knowing. Of the array of things heretofore presented I suspect those who make this cognitive request of life would like the Niccolo da Uzzano bust. Others of them might prefer the little haiku which capsules for their comprehension the duality and unity of life. They would, I think, find Gudrun's lament and Goya's "Cronos" without enough external significance, even though I can imagine some of them trying to erect for the latter a kind of mythic framework about the eternal truth of devouring death.

There is a historically minded person of the cognitive sort who likes to find in art a habit of mind that reflects its time. Seeking to understand history, such a sort of man finds art a reflection of a past. He need not have something definitely said about the time; he does not look at Renaissance portraits for the costumes of the people pictured or for the background architecture, say, though these are interesting to him, but for what seems to be admired, disliked, recognized by the painter. So Shakespeare becomes an "Elizabethan" and his world an Elizabethan world, and the claim is made that Shakespeare cannot be understood except in reference to that world and its habits of mind. Such a way of viewing art is, of course, a common way of viewing it in colleges; there have always been, I imagine, more historians of literature on college faculties than there have been literary critics or theorists of art. History, the knowledge of the past, is more substantiable and more objective (thus "honorable") than the subjective choices of theory and of criticism. Even the critic, working with the habits of art of his own time and expecting of art what his time expects, would be regarded as somewhat narrow if he looked at ancient or foreign stories or statues and found them ineffective because they did not have as their main designs and motions and tones the manners he was used to. The critic could, I imagine, be justified in saying he got very little emotional impact from a Chinese portrait because it did not use light and shade and so present the looming force to the critic's psyche that the critic gets from a three-dimensional portrait in space. He would only be telling the truth about himself if he said so, no doubt, but to judge the quality on that disappointed expectation and to fail to respond to the Chinese manner would be thought ignorant. To object to the old Mesopotamian *Gilgamesh* because it doesn't seem like Joyce's *Ulysses* would likewise be regarded, I am afraid, as a naïveté of the first order. Such mistakes about Chinese painting and early stories are, fortunately, not often made today except by the young and inexperienced. Historical setting is important to any critic who, by rearrangement of his expectations, can learn to respond to what is there to respond to, and then, on a new basis, found his judgments. Only a more particular sort of person, however, would regard the historical difference as the major importance of the art. One can hear him speaking of the Kutenai tale, not as a good tale in anyone's language, but as anthropologically interesting, as revealing Kutenai habits of mind and culture, and of Tu Fu's poem as an example of the Chinese, essentially Cha'an, point of view.

It is not a very long jump from liking to know and to understand as an end in life to liking to be a better man. Improvement as a policy and as an endless end is not one of the least popular bents of the modern mind. It comes in two forms, of course, individual improvement and social improvement. These join at a point which says if everyone were better, society would be better. The emphasis of each will differ, however, as the Jeffersonian individual man differs from the recent Democrat, whose eye is on many men; and the artistic judgment of each may be expected to shift accordingly.

Those who wish individual improvement will ask of art not only comprehension but some kind of purgation of the psyche. As I have suggested before, tragedy and comedy both may have this effect. Undoubtedly pictures of the horrid that make one revolt from the horrid are purgative. The army venereal disease pictures, various traffic department pictures of automobile accidents, are gauged to produce purgation alone, but some such end is one of the effects of many pieces of art. Both Goya's painting of Cronos and Gudrun's lament may, by presenting the wrong, shift one's attitudes toward the right. The danger here, of course, is that by excess of impact or intensity such pieces of art may bring the repudiation of calling them melodrama, as the reaction of many young soldiers to VD pictures may be scorn—though one can hardly believe the scorners will not, in spite of scorn, remember caution.

The psychoanalytic critics, who believe art is good by its straightening out of unresolved repressions in the subconscious, are, of course, a therapeutic group. One can hardly avoid saying that mental "sickness" is bad and mental health good, so that the psychoanalytic critics become major defenders of moral improvement. Indeed, psychoanalysis is a great moral industry.

The socially minded of the improvement or moral bent can, I suppose, be called "humanists." The term implies a concern with man and for man; the goal they can find is human betterment. Though some of them are religious men who have faith in an afterlife, and though some of them act for other men in order to guarantee their own stations in that afterlife, the overriding emphasis of their thought is on improving this world. Such improvement is the expressed motive of politicians and of political parties. Such improvement is the justification for education and for teachers. Such improvement is the advertised purpose of many major corporations—better things for better living—and of major foundations, labor unions, and so on. Though one may very cynically believe protestations do not reflect motives and do not issue in actions, there are a high proportion of the protesters who are at bottom motivated by socially moral purpose. And a high proportion of these, men we would admire if the capacity for admiration be in us, would, I think, judge art finally by what they conceive its social value. What the social effect of a piece of art may be is not at all easy to guess, and too often the humanist may be led to plunk for piety of a sort and to repudiate what at first seems destructive. The scorn that some other temperaments feel for the humanist one stems from the failure of the humanist to think hard enough; he is inclined to accept sentimental idealism too easily; he is too prone to favor things that seem "encouraging." Yet the thoughtful of him may see through the falsities of false hope, the exaggerations of sympathy for the downtrodden, the warmths of reward for virtue. He may have, as I suggested in the chapter on social effects, to depend at last on the judgment of integrity, may enlarge what that means to the kind of balanced view of all sides of a situation that one meets in Donatello's bust or in such profound comprehension as Faulkner showed in *Go Down, Moses.* It would not be the pleasure afforded by the internal fitting together of many pieces but the honesty of comprehension that straightens out the mind.

At one moment the humanist might applaud C. Day Lewis for his poem about a new day, for this turning forward. Yet he might find it too protestant and hortative to be a "great" poem. Somewhere here, however, in the value for healthy attitudes, no matter whether developed by repulsions or promotions or by the middle way of understanding, the humanist may finally decide that a piece of art is worthy. He is a very large class and among his various shades of judgment includes, I should imagine, a majority of the educated. Indeed, one might guess that the qualities the humanist admires may be found prominent in the world's remembered art.

The humanists of the past, as I have suggested, have too often been mixed up with "do-gooders," with those who held irrational moral views, with the second-rate pious. Partially in reaction against the failures of humanism, partially as a result of those discoveries about the nature of the world which we lump under the heading of science, the last hundred years has seen the gradual development of a new bent. It is a bent not yet possible to name, I think. Darwin's hypothesis gave it its first great impetus in European thought. Nietzsche's famous "God is dead" expressed one of its tenets. Mark Twain was subject to it, for instance. The First World War made evident some of its contentions. These center, perhaps, about the lack of justice in the world, not the lack of inhuman order but the lack of reward for merit. One of the first reactions was a kind of stoic response: men must bear up without expectation. If you picked the three major "thoughtful" writers in English of the first half of the twentieth century, I fancy you might come on Conrad, Hemingway, and Faulkner (the next rank would include Joyce and Eliot, the first without a position, the second regressive). These three all express a doctrine of fortitude in face of an indifferent universe: Conrad from before the world war and stressing "solidarity" among men; Hemingway protesting self-control and bravery against "they," the nameless forces; and Faulkner using various words like "pride" and "humility" and "love" but coming out before his Nobel Prize speech most often with the word "endure," which he altered in that speech from "endure" to "prevail." All three changed their techniques of structure, following what Hemingway expressed as the refusal to put a "wow" at the end of their stories; though Faulkner often did indulge himself so, and a Hemingway story like "The Short Happy Life of Francis Macomber" ends with a wife shooting her husband. Their new techniques led to comprehension rather than to "effect," led to a balance of pro and con about people rather than to black and white judgments.

European painters and musicians were the first to rebel against the humanist and hedonist art of the nineteenth century. The abstract and atonal movements were powered by the struggle for "purity" of appeal by the nature of the medium. So architects turned from decoration and memorial shapes to structures dependent on the nature of materials and, less successfully, to design by function. The philosophers and literary men of Europe, though some who are no longer much remembered experimented with nonsense, were well behind other sorts of artists, and indeed seemed to see the loss of divine help and universal justice as a crying matter. It is dubious that men like Sartre and Camus caught up to the intellectual maturity of Conrad or Hemingway.

Conrad, Hemingway, and Faulkner remained humanist, without illusion, they would have said, and achieving perhaps only a sort of holding position, tempered by Faulkner's "it will be long." Many Europeans, distraught by the failure of the Old World view and hunting for some sort of security, succumbed to the other major intellectual strain of our century, the scientific. Though scientists nowadays begin to realize that the schemes they make are no less subjective than those of the humanist, they do have a test of verifiability, ultimately gauged, of course, by the subjective human eye. Science seems objective. Objectivity means a lack of contamination by human feelings and wishes and so means something "dehumanized." Thus a major attitude of the past generation has been—and still is—the repudiation of all that Holden Caulfield, the teen-age hero of Salinger's *The Catcher in the Rye,* would call "phony." What this has meant for art has been the attempt to get away from what one could react to in a specifically human way. In music, melody, singability, has gone; meter has left in it no foot-beat; climax has gone; even in popular music the "rousing" effect of the old improvisation of Benny Goodman times has given way to the "cool" relations of tone and phrase. The newest music is not arranged by the old harmonics and phraseology one had learned to be accustomed to, that one could "like." Even the clear formalities of Bach are gone. One is not expected, I think, to "like" contemporary experimental music; perhaps one can be "fascinated" by it. Its endurability remains for time to decide. Meanwhile, the music of the computer, where tones may be expanded and diminished and changed by a planned intricacy of computation, is now to be explored.

In painting, from the time when Kandinsky left behind any shape one could ally with a known shape from the real, the abstract and, later, nonrepresentational painters have worked on the effects of color and shape as color and shape, as the musicians have worked with unconnotative sound. Mondrian's picture seems to me one end of such a search. Many who have looked at painting have learned to avoid hunting for sources from life or implications into life. Some nowadays say, however, that the exploration of color and shape and texture has come close to going as far as it can go; there is a reversion to paintings of "things," represented at the moment by the painting of relatively meaningless objects, such as rows of soup cans or the letter "A." One can invent for such pictures a social implication: this is our crass materialist civilization. I doubt this as an intended implication; the pictures seem to be taken as new, often violently colored arrangements of shape, and for me they seem to have a half-jocular tone, for I cannot conceive one taking them as seriously significant and must therefore conceive them as being done with a good deal of tongue in the cheek.

To dehumanize literature is not easy, for words have references, and humankind has some sort of reaction pro or con toward most things one can refer to. True, a geology textbook may be pretty dehumanized, but it doesn't seem much like art. After the First World War there were some trials made of association by sound rather than by reference and a brief flurry of quite incomprehensible writing by men allied with the game-players of the absurd, the Dadaists. James Joyce, after experimenting with various techniques, all finally representational, went on in *Finnegans Wake* to try to evoke the language of the half-restrained, half-dream state. Perhaps something like X. J. Kennedy's poem is as "pure" as literature can be.

After the Second World War and the general spread of the existential denial of importance to life, there has grown up a second literature of the "absurd." The tenets have been the failure of language to communicate, the negation of "personality" as a breeder of response, and an attention to purely mechanical effects. There has been relatively little fiction in this mode but a good deal of theater. Theater without significance except for its pure stimulation of eye and muscular empathy can be found in the old vaudeville and French circus turns: there is extremely little meaning in acrobatics and almost none in a song-and-dance team. Samuel Beckett and Ionesco have made use of such methods in part. They and their various confreres, however, have also wished to purvey a series of positions about war, society, language, and the cosmos, and beyond the theatric vitality of the characters in *Waiting for Godot* or the theatric trick of peopling a stage with invisible actors in Ionesco's *The Chairs* one finds the "message," the presentation of meaninglessness which, the playwrights insist, challenges the audience to create in revulsion its own meaning. Unfortunately no actor can so dehumanize himself that he does not convey a personality to the audience. The pure mechanical theater has not yet been presented by those who profess the tenets of "absurdity"; there may yet be a way to make an art in words as nonreferent and as free of evocation of feelings as nonrepresentational painting and the music of no melody and no meter and no key; it has so far not been found.

Whether such art will long endure, whether it can escape in any verbal medium the tendency of men to humanize, to transform the motion of diatoms under microscopic vision, say, into motivated and animist and at last human activity, I do not know. It is true, I think, that there is a very powerful effect that comes from the sight of "rich" colors set side by side in a not too symmetrical arrangement, as there is a very powerful effect that comes from a simple musical arpeggio if set in silence and in space (I remember a guide singing one in the Baptistery at Pisa and the echoes merging into a sonorous chord). Surely we have learned to react to "pure" sound and "pure" color and shape; whether we can react to verbal "purity" I do not know, for I find it hard to imagine what that would be – except for the nonsense syllables of some recent popular singers, where music dominates words, after all.

It is hard to ascribe a purpose to this scientific—or formalist—temper of mind. I suppose it is based on a kind of honest recognition of the state of man. Conrad, Hemingway, Faulkner—and many, many others—surmounted the shock of this recognition to concentrate on what can most easily be phrased as the "simple interests of the human heart." Perhaps this was a regression to the falsities of the past; perhaps, contrariwise, it is the only "out" for mankind. Meanwhile, there are many who feel that the only good art is that which refuses the chance of human sentimentality, who feel that such art devotes itself to praise of the superhuman cosmos, as Fra Angelico devoted his art to praise of what he felt divine. This "purist" criterion is not, today, unpopular.

These four temperaments or bents or ways of looking at life—the hedonist, the cognitive, the moral, the scientific—seem to me the major bents of mankind today. Perhaps one should add the religious. Certainly in the past and in much of the world today the religious setting and religious purpose of art have been major. There have been a great many genuinely religious men and an often greater number who have professed a religious attitude, however their actions belied them. In part the religious man has been of a cognitive sort, coming to know the truth; in part he has been a moral man, living the life of virtue. Yet his special sign has been, I suppose, a devotion of himself outward beyond himself toward something as center of the universe. Insofar as he wishes his own salvation he is a hedonist, of course, whose happiness may be delayed to another life. Of such sort are all Buddhists, for instance. Insofar as he is a genuine devotee—"for the glory of God"—he forms a fifth sort of bent, allied by devotion outward to the social humanist, but less social than individualist and not necessarily "moral" in one sense at all. It is not easy to discover what such a man would ask of art. The Zuni use art as a means of helping the divine forces to perform their functions, and the criterion of propriety—"done right," whatever that exactly means—is perhaps dominant. The personal salvationist has regarded art as a means to induce proper feelings. This was true of Phidias' forty-foot Athena, and of Asiatic Buddhas, and of statues of Christ and of the saints. I suppose one could say efficacy was a criterion, the effect of the piece of art in inducing the proper attitude. Yet how will this operate? I suppose upon one's human feelings in a way one can ally with the purgative and therapeutic. If the divine be thought of as orderly and static, then one mark of religious art will be its order and symmetry, and many pieces of religious art have been of this sort. The expression of surety and serenity and control has marked such statuary. The splendor and magnificence and omnipotence of divinities have been expressed by the magnificence of the religious objects, and what might at first seem likely, the simple and unitary, has been decorated by intricacy, by gold and jewels. The artist and his patron have devoted worldly things to otherworldly ends. Yet such glorification has always had a few simplistic critics who have regarded such display as vulgar, and the "Puritan" reaction has occurred elsewhere than in European society. The reverse of magnificence, the raw, frightening power of divinity, the old Hebraic sense of Jehovah as angry, has been expressed in several religions by the picturing of horror, the Gorgon mask, the Kali, or destructive aspect of the Hindu Shiva, the famous blocklike, skull-strewn demonic death deity of the Aztecs, and so on. This is the "scare" motif of the fire and brimstone sermon of some Christian sects. Efficacy has been sought by other means, too: by the expression in the art of the feelings of the divinity, so that the suffering saint, the commiserating Bodhisattva, the agonized Christ have been pictorial and literary symbols of the humanity of divine folk. The god has become the hero.

All such—and many other—attributes of religious work are to be judged in a religious way by their external meanings, by their propaganda effect, I suppose. To the religious bent a demand for such an effect is a legitimate one, yet I find many religious folk ambivalent; they can look at the devotional object as a religious symbol and bow before it and then judge it by criteria no different from the criteria other bents would use. Thus the artistic demands of the religious man are not easily separable from the demands of other bents, though the religious demands may be. And one can hardly believe that the religious artist's sense of order and relationship has been different from that of the lay artist, however his intention has been cognitive or therapeutic.

Of our four major bents, then, the hedonist will seek pleasure, the cognitive some kind of comprehension, the moral the therapeutic. What will the scientific seek? I suspect order and arrangement, and arrangement rather static than dynamic. Thus the New Criticism as a form of analysis tended to hunt for relationships, patterns, alliances of meaning, and for this reason has fitted very well into the scientific, analytic, and intellectual temper prominent in this century.

Which of the pieces of art these bents will prefer cannot be suggested neatly and clearly. Surely the hedonist bent will prefer pleasure, but whether from the strong impact of Gudrun's lament or the play of Donne's ideas or the sudden outthrust and hope of C. Day Lewis' poem or the feeling of unity of Tu Fu's would be hard to tell—

or from the craftsmanly finish of Kennedy's. Whatever the means, his test will be the pleasure he finds.

The man who wishes truth and external meaning, however, will be less hard put here. The haiku and Donatello's bust will be the most cognitive and significant, perhaps, for though Gudrun's lament is historical—or at least old—and has a temper not of our time but suitable to a Viking age, it is not a poem which enlarges out to the world or one especially connotative. Donne's poem is too much a stunt of the brain, intellectual but not substantial fodder for thought. Perhaps Tu Fu's suggests comprehension of the world, yet it is so much a mood at last that the cognitive man might regard the poem as a little too "aesthetic." And Lewis' poem might seem polemic, more a call to action than to contemplation, more social than individual. It is for these reasons I think the cognitive man would choose the thought of the haiku.

The critic who wishes to be improved might feel that the strong experience of "The First Lay of Gudrun" was wholesome, but it does not, as the story does, put Brynhild's violence of heart before the murder of Sigurd, and the tragic purgation does not come clear. Tu Fu's cosmic view is quieting, thrusts down to their place the excesses of man, and against the others has perhaps restorative quality. Donne's wit has little external meaning; though his viewpoint seems sane, his issue seems hardly serious. Lewis is driving the individual into a social dawn, one feels; he is speaking *to,* not crowing. And Kennedy's poem, denying both thought and feeling, is so slight an experience in any but a visual and "artistic" way that it is hard to find a means of improvement in it. None of these are *immoral* poems, none destructive, none sentimental, though Gudrun's feeling may seem melodramatic to gentle temperaments.

Certain sorts of humanists may find Lewis' social consciousness attractive and the vigor of his verse effective on their psyches. Others, more quietist, may prefer Tu Fu's sense of all being in it together. And still others may feel the experience of Gudrun, shared in the small way it can be by the reader, increases that sense of human solidarity and sympathy which is a great part of humanist value.

The scientific temper might find Donne's intellectual play and Kennedy's visual sights the most honest and the least self-involving. In one way or another the others ask emotion and value. Though the high finish of Tu Fu's world might make a neat scheme, yet its promotion of a view might destroy its self-sufficiency.

The religious, I think, would find Tu Fu's poem the closest to their sentiments, since it has something of the tone of "vanity, vanity," yet it has too little sense of devotion to be, for the Western world, religious. And now the kind of religious man he was underneath his religiosity would come into play.

Now, perhaps, such clarity as there was heretofore is destroyed before the multiplicity of shades within each temperament. All one can ask is: "Is there one thing a piece of literature *has* to give you for you to be satisfied?" Only each individual can answer that, for himself and often after very arduous examination of his likes.

In sum, then, the bent of one's mind and character, the kind of ends one seeks in life will declare at last the final criterion by which one judges art. This is not at all to say that a badly organized thing that yet has a therapeutic effect will be admired by the moral temperament. The major artistic qualities and meanings still remain as first criteria, but between two things roughly approximate in order and experience and being, one man will choose one and another man another by the emphasis of some other quality apt to his bent.

Men are, of course, inconsistent, and it is easy to say that an individual humanist type might inconsistently love impersonal and "scientific" art. Yet one may wonder here about his humanism. There is, so far as I know, no valid study of such inconsistencies among men. I should guess we finally become more consistent than inconsistent and that when we do so we can look back and see that "all the time" one's bent was really there though hidden by the mistakes of consciousness.

There is, I think, no way of saying one bent is better than another. I suppose a final test would be the capacity of the bent to keep going and to keep mankind going. None of these bents seems to be destructive or self-destructive; all will promote survival; even the genuinely religious has seemed to do so. Of the "scientific" we have yet insufficient evidence. We would not, of course, want one bent to dominate others, for the diversity of life and the potentialities of humankind would thereby be diminished. We would not want, then, to judge one bent "better" than another; though birds of a feather may flock together, warfare among feathers would seem to us at last both dangerous and absurd. Thus a man's taste, dependent finally on his bent, is his own and honorable, and the consistency of his character his badge of honor.

Thus at last each man must make his choice himself. Plato might have dictated in the name of one truth and one character. I should urge no final truth but consistency, and thus the title of this treatise remains "The Choices of Criticism."

CHAPTER 10

The Place of Criticism

ON THE way to final judgment there are for the critic, it seems to me, the areas of examination I have tried to suggest. The critic must consider the experience he goes through and all its meanings as experience. He must consider the order of the piece and the meanings that purveys. He must consider the integrity of the piece as a work of art. He must consider of what sorts these elements are. He can, in some way or another, make an estimate of them as more or less good or bad or moderate. Some critics will refuse to go further than this, for further than this reaches into opinion, and opinion seems to them dishonest. Even if the critic goes further into the pleasures and cognitions and purgations of the piece—which may come under the heading of the meanings of the experience—he may remain still essentially descriptive: "it has these qualities." Yet what we at last ask of him is to take some final stand: what value has this thing for human life—*in your opinion?* The critic exposes himself even by his reticences; he cannot escape the light; he cannot escape being judged himself.

A defense can be given, I think, for never losing sight of what one can hold as perfection. Nothing may ever come up to that—oh, there may be some pieces we could not imagine improving, but few and mostly small ones—but the recognition that perfection is unattainable may sober off our doctrinaire insistences and allow us to make considerate appraisals. So we may see Shakespeare not as the most impeccable though perhaps the greatest playwright; we need not always defend his structure or his logic or always, even, that phraseology which is often so extraordinary an enlargement of our experience. Homer can nod, and we need not feel we are lessening his stature by pointing out the humanity of his nods. And what could perfection be? Would yours and mine be the same? From the point of view of those who like order perfection may be bought, for the hedonist and humanist, at the cost of external meanings and even of internal ones.

We are inclined to say, I think, "perfect of its kind," as I should be inclined to say of the statue of Buddha and of Basho's little poem and of Emily Dickinson's, too. "Of its kind," however, suggests there are other kinds and other perfections, and that, therefore, "perfection" is a word for a unison of qualities only one kind of critic will admire and can be no universal word. Yet what we each see as perfection will show us strengths and weaknesses and make more reasonable and more useful what we say.

Judgment, then, becomes a compromise, a judicious pointing out of the relative values of the many attributes of a piece of art. To be judicious may seem an authoritative and admirable way to be. One takes this piece of work apart and shows here good, there not so good; one may even point out that those who especially like this quality may applaud the piece and those who especially like that will be disappointed: the formalist approves its consistency of structure, the hedonist disapproves its failure to evoke feeling. Some critics will be happy to feel themselves able to "keep their heads" in this way. Their services to others will be very considerable.

Yet can one man manage the thoroughly judicious? And do we want him to? I have a suspicion without much evidence except what critics have said and left unsaid that the individual will tend to find in a piece of art especially those qualities which interest him most; here his feelings will be most easily stimulated and his mind perhaps be most aware. He may well neglect in response and in sight what he values less. What I am suggesting is that a bent is a bias, and we are all bent and biased. To be truly judicious, then, becomes difficult; to become so we may force ourselves into insincerity. Perhaps, then, we may more admire the man who defends his bias, who takes a stand. Because there is some connection between conviction and effectiveness, the man with a strong central bias may be more effective on us. We need not accept, but if we hear conviction speaking, we may learn more and "see" more.

If I felt there *were* an answer, a certainly good and a certainly bad, I should not speak as I do, of course. Then I should be forced to try to show the way to certainty. The human psyche is not a computer, however: it makes mistakes and its memory can never "dump" and begin afresh. And no models are identical. Thus each alone may reach its own certainty, and all others learn and reassess from it on the way to their individual certainties.

Criticism must be based on such breadth of analysis of what is in the piece of art as one can manage. It must be as judicious in its judgment of this property and that as it can manage. It must, however, come from an individual psyche and an individual bent, and no two men's experience of a piece of art will be identical. The more one comes toward judgment out of analysis, the more one's individual taste will emphasize and overlook.

Yet the individual judgment can approach its own consistency, can understand the implications of its own consistency, and can try for its own integrity.

All this may seem to imply the most anarchic sort of pluralism. As I have pointed out before, men are more alike than different, however, and what they like and dislike, with somewhat the same amount of sensitivity and thought by each of them, will not result in utterly anarchic judgment. There will be a rough consensus. It is only with art of relatively high merit that the major differences will show. With lesser things the criteria of art or good art will suffice; with the better ones there will come into play the choices of philosophic bent. Tastes cannot be disputed, but tastes can be understood and their implications viewed and their logics established. And here, when we are talking about what "really matters" to us, we need the most awareness and the most integrity.

For even in casual conversation what we are talking about is the nature of human life, and what we think about that, and how to manage it, is a sober pursuit, even if we decide at last to take it all as a jocular affair. Art is about life after all, even when it seems most distant from it, and of all the arts, because far and away the most psychically complex, literature speaks most warmly to the concern of men.

About such speech the critic must at last speak himself. How he speaks, on what premises of human value, is his choice.

In the long run, society must demand we all in some way speak, for how we speak, act, think, feel forms our society and gives it being. An aesthetic judgment becomes finally a philosophic judgment, and a philosophic judgment turns into a political judgment. Human society cannot survive without political judgment, and no man can long survive without society. The chain of relations here may seem to be made of fragile and undemonstrable links, and I would be hard put to demonstrate their solidity, but I am sure that what we see in art, and our opinion of it, is a factor in our characters, a formulator of our attitudes, and a shaper of our response to all significant things.

The better our responses, the better our lives and the better our societies. Thus criticism, the making consciously consistent of our taste, is a necessary activity in civilization. One's choice is his character, and his character his choice.

Notes

Notes

Chapter 2

1. "To Daffodils" by Robert Herrick, to be found in *The Oxford Book of English Verse,* Oxford University Press, New York, 1939.
2. Haiku by Onitsura, from *An Introduction to Haiku* by Harold G. Henderson. Copyright 1958 by Harold G. Henderson. Reprinted by permission of Doubleday & Company, Inc.
3. From *Kutenai Tales* by Franz Boas, Bureau of American Ethnology Bulletin 59, U.S. Government Printing Office, Washington, D. C., 1918.

Chapter 3

1. Haiku by Shiki from *An Introduction to Haiku.* (See Chapter 2, Note 2.)
2. Sonnet XXIX by William Shakespeare, *The Oxford Shakespeare,* Oxford University Press, New York, 1943.
3. From the Poetics of Aristotle, to be found in *An Introduction to Aristotle,* edited by Richard McKeon, Modern Library, New York, 1947.
4. "I saw a Chapel All of Gold" by William Blake, to be found in *Immortal Poems of the English Language,* edited by Oscar Williams, Washington Square Press, Inc., New York, 1960.
5. From "The Scoffers" by William Blake, *ibid.*
6. "When I Heard the Learn'd Astronomer" by Walt Whitman, from *Leaves of Grass,* Modern Library, New York, 1940.

Chapter 4

1. Chapter V from *In Our Time* by Ernest Hemingway, The Scribner Library, Charles Scribner's Sons, New York, by permission of the publishers.

Chapter 5

1. From Sonnet XXX and Sonnet CXVI by William Shakespeare. (See Chapter 3, Note 2.)
2. "Essay on Criticism" by Alexander Pope, Part 2, line 325, in *Complete Poetical Works,* edited by H. W. Boynton, Houghton Mifflin Company, Cambridge, Mass., 1903.
3. From *Go Down, Moses* by William Faulkner, The Modern Library, New York, 1955.
4. Sonnet XXIX by William Shakespeare. (See Chapter 3, Note 2.)
5. Haiku by Basho, from *An Introduction to Haiku.* (See Chapter 2, Note 2.)
6. "The Soul Selects Her Own Society" by Emily Dickinson, to be found in *Immortal Poems of the English Language.* (See Chapter 3, Note 4.)
7. From "The Isles of Greece" by Lord Byron, to be found in *The Oxford Book of English Verse.* (See Chapter 2, Note 1.)

Chapter 6

1. "Woman" by Oliver Goldsmith, to be found in *The Oxford Book of English Verse* and *Immortal Poems of the English Language.* (See Chapter 2, Note 1 and Chapter 3, Note 4.)
2. From "The Psalm of Life" by Henry Wadsworth Longfellow, *The Complete Poetical Works of Henry Wadsworth Longfellow,* Houghton Mifflin Company, Cambridge, Mass., 1893.
3. From "To Althea, from Prison" by Richard Lovelace, to be found in *The Oxford Book of English Verse* and *Immortal Poems of the English Language.* (See Chapter 2, Note 1 and Chapter 3, Note 4.)

Chapter 7

1. Chant from "Zuni Ritual Poetry" by Ruth L. Bunzel, in The *47th Annual Report* of the Bureau of American Ethnology, 1929–1930, U.S. Government Printing Office, Washington, D. C.
2. "Animula" by Thomas Stearns Eliot, from *Collected Poems 1909–1962* by T. S. Eliot, copyright, 1936, by Harcourt, Brace & World, Inc.; copyright, 1963, 1964, by T. S. Eliot. Reprinted by permission of the publisher.

Chapter 8

1. "Of the Lamentation of Gudrun over Sigurd dead," translated by William Morris, to be found in *Volsungasaga: The Story of Volsungs and Niblungs,* with a new introduction by Robert W. Gutman, Collier Books, New York, 1962.
2. "Love's Deity" by John Donne, to be found in *Immortal Poems of the English Language.* (See Chapter 3, Note 4.)
3. Haiku by Basho, from *An Introduction to Haiku.* (See Chapter 2, Note 2.)
4. "Rest from Loving" by Cecil Day Lewis, from *Collected Poems of C. Day Lewis,* Jonathan Cape with the Hogarth Press, London, 1954. Reprinted by permission of the author.
5. "Night at the Apartments" by Tu Fu. Translated by Nathan Sivin.
6. "Nude Descending a Staircase," from the book *Nude Descending a Staircase,* by X. J. Kennedy, copyright 1960. Reprinted by permission of Doubleday & Company, Inc.

Chapter 9

1. From "The Tiger" by William Blake, to be found in *The Oxford Book of English Verse* and *Immortal Poems of the English Language.* (See Chapter 2, Note 1 and Chapter 3, Note 4.)
2. From "In Time of Pestilence" by Thomas Nashe, to be found in *The Oxford Book of English Verse.* (See Chapter 2, Note 1.)
3. From "The Sick Rose" by William Blake, to be found in William Blake, *Poetical Works,* Oxford University Press, New York, 1914.